Studio SKLIM

Evolving Techne

Studio SKLIM

Evolving Techne

Contents

6   Limbo
10 Community Recognition
16 Introduction

27 Voids Café
Singapore

41 Deloitte Center for the Edge
Singapore

59 Hansha Reflection House
Japan

83 Rattan Clouds
Singapore

93 Verdant Spine Office
Singapore

107 +Pavilion
Singapore

121 Brick Bakery
Singapore

135 Ombré Patchwork Apartment
Singapore

151 Bamboo Umbrella Pavilions
Thailand

159 Modern High School International
India

184 Lo-Hi Tech Material Research
190 Studio SKLIM
192 Kevin Lim
194 Accolades
196 Acknowledgments
198 Project Credits

Limbo
Three Forms of Material Depth

01

Take the Modern High School International project in India. A fat box with a core in the back that frees the plan from inconvenient obstacles. An explicit free plan at the ground floor, another free plan under the roof, and a series of implicit free plans in-between, free from the requirements of ground and roof, and, more importantly, free from the demand of expressing freedom. The typical plan is deliberately left free of unwanted outer determinations, as if suspended, thus rendered generic, on hold, and surrounded by a completely unconstrained envelope—regularly gridded and irregularly perforated. And yet, despite this freeing effort, the massing studies introduce a whole series of modes of spatial difference within, atrium-gaps that disturb the peace and muteness of the generic spatial organization achieved. The envelope, in this paradoxical context, operates at two conceptually conflicting registers of depth: skin depth (the depth of ornament and character articulation) and spatial depth (the depth of organizational and programmatic specification), confusing by literally stretching the gridded rhythms of the former into the circulatory serpentines of the latter through wildly varied modularity. Material depth in its elastic cavernous form.

02

Or take the Hansha Reflection House in Japan. A long and compact box, forcefully elongated by the proportions and frontage of the plot, containing front and back rooms and a patio in the middle, under a transversal, slightly pitched roof. A self-sufficient organization that, given its interiorised exterior, does not inevitably depend upon the front and back sides for ventilation and illumination. Flat, opaque façades (shiny and dark as well) with particularly small openings are manifestations of this autonomy. The unpretentious containment of the mass is only disrupted by the alleged pragmatics of accommodating the car at the front, generating a setback that folds the volume and shrinks the ground level, turning the mass into surface. Counteracting with this setback, the volume appears to violently protrude above, but it only extends out of its supposed size and form (the one that is symmetrical in size to that of the back) at its corners. The outburst at the corners is, in turn, neutralized by the inward receding of the central iconic window, the thickness of which further invades the interior and furnishes it with an unexpected intrusion. The compactness of the mass thus turns into a topological envelope, and the potentially mute façade into a faceted emblem. Material depth in its pliant, dancing form.

03

Or else, take the Deloitte Center for the Edge or the Voids Café, or the Verdant Spine Office, all in Singapore. The furniture extrudes upward from the floors or downward from the ceilings. Booths are carved into these extrusions, seats and seating areas cut sections away, plant pots excavate them, flowerpots cantilever out of them, lighting cavities are hollowed in, sinks and other kitchen artifacts are carved into them, shelves stick out, and magazine stands unfold and infold their finishing. Sharply contrasted tabletops are laid out on them as if they were thick mantles. Smooth finishes are unrolled onto them as if they were impenetrable carpets. Continuous surfaces are split apart as if they were drawn, painted, or coated onto one another, while completely alien ones are merged with fillets in all directions, as if it all belonged to a single continuum. Corners are treated as sharp, paper-like edges and punctual, multidirectional light is used to increase the loss of directionality of things and intensify the loss of the thingness of things. Although presented (and crafted) in catalogues of specific and functional prototypical forms, objects, and artifacts, their presence is liquified in the wandering population of space, thus treated as a medium of indeterminacy and play. Material depth in its erratic, playful form.

Material depth is thus given idiosyncratic form and is tightly occupied. Space, in turn, is rendered as the (charged) leftover hedonistic limbo of architecture, its surplus.

Ciro Najle
Professor in Practice at Rensselaer Polytechnic Institute.
Professor and former Dean of Architecture at Universidad Torcuato di Tella.
Previously Diploma Unit Master and Director of Landscape Urbanism at the Architectural Association.
Visiting Professor at Harvard, Cornell, Columbia, Berlage, Universidad de Buenos Aires.

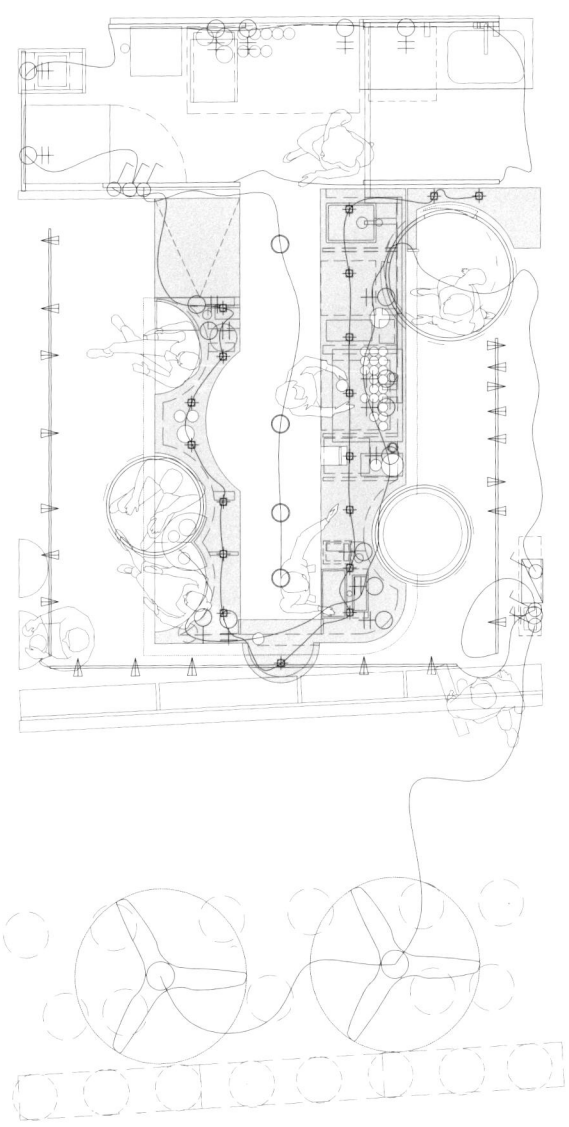

Community Recognition

Highest of Standards

Kevin Lim and Studio SKLIM set the highest standards when it comes to commitment and owning the project. Their interpretation of the client's expectations are very accurate. We were pleasantly surprised to see how well they handled and coordinated with an internationally diverse team. They added value to the project through innovative thoughts and out-of-the-box thinking. Their research of India and the education system was not only impressive but also very insightful. Their designs subtly infuse local contemporary styles onto an international palette. Kevin Lim is a passionate and knowledgeable individual who has his roots to the ground. A rare virtue in these days!

Smt. Nirmala Birla
Chairperson, Modern High School International
Kolkata, India

Encapsulating the Ethos

Our vision for the Deloitte Center for the Edge space was not merely architectural; it was about embodying the essence of our mission as a futures think tank. Studio SKLIM, under Kevin Lim's brilliant direction, translated this vision into a tangible form, creating an environment that provokes thought, inspires innovation, and fosters meaningful connections with our clients. Their work on our space is a testament to the power of design in encapsulating the ethos of forward-thinking and strategic advisement.

The +Pavilion project showcased a ground-up collective drive for sustainability, merging Studio SKLIM's design expertise with a wide partnership, including our team. This hands-on approach, favoring a tangible model over reports, engaged thousands, making sustainability not just a concept but an experience. This project vividly demonstrated how complex ideas can be brought to life, ensuring sustainability's principles are both seen and felt.

Our collaboration with Studio SKLIM has been pivotal, transforming our dialogue about the future into tangible spaces that reflect the change we envision. This partnership has been crucial in our mission to foster a sustainable and innovative future, proving the power of design in achieving our goals.

Duleesha Kulasooriya
Innovation Leader, Deloitte Asia Pacific
Managing Director, Deloitte Center for the Edge
Singapore

A Vision for the Future

As a New York–based artist and entrepreneur working with multiple types of materials, I am always seeking innovative ways to design and create new, eye-pleasing, and functional products and effects that people will want to use and interact with in their daily lives. To accomplish this, I sometimes employ old methods and technologies such as welding, carpentry, and sewing. However, I also embrace new technologies, utilizing multiple CAD design software and various platforms of 3D printing.

We live in an amazing time where the crossroads of the old meets the new. The world has changed enormously in the last 40 years, creating many new opportunities for individuals and companies who are willing to venture into uncharted territories to explore fresh ideas and visions that diverge from the past.

When I think of Studio SKLIM, they are one of those companies. The first thing that comes to mind is their dedication to sustainability and simplicity. The way they seamlessly weave older materials in new ways creates an aesthetic that harmonizes with the environment of their projects—a mindset that I deeply resonate with.

I admire the tactile quality of their work; many of their projects serve as a wellspring of inspiration for me.
I firmly believe they represent a company of the future, and I eagerly anticipate witnessing their continued innovation and growth.

Scott Taylor
Visual artist, utilizing 3D printing for art, design, and fashion applications. Previously an event producer, nightclub owner, and a bartender at the original Studio 54.
New York, USA

Making a Difference

Studio SKLIM is an innovative and forward-thinking architecture studio. I find their approach to researching and developing strategies to incorporate "slowness" into their architectural practice particularly intriguing.

One of their earlier projects, Rattan Clouds, demonstrated an early sensibility toward materiality as the studio reinterpreted rattan, a traditional Southeast Asian material. They created modular capsules adaptable for seating, storage, display, and lighting, collaborating with artisans and employing traditional bending techniques.

Studio SKLIM continued this practice trajectory by working with materials through projects like +Pavilion and Lo-Hi Tech. Both projects evolved from the same sensibility toward materials and ideas from "primitive" technologies, with interesting provocations that impact our approach to building.

+Pavilion and Lo-Hi Tech showcase Studio SKLIM's collaboration with local artisans to design and fabricate biocomposites, as well as to explore primitive knowledge systems for sustainable solutions. In this context, "slowness" encompasses more than just the creation of new building materials; it represents a different approach to relating to people and respecting the Earth and her resources. This concept of "slowness" serves as a form of defiance against the fast-paced development and short lifespans of buildings in Singapore, with which we are familiar.

My interpretation of Studio SKLIM's concept of "slowness" is influenced by my research on urban participation during times of climate crisis, where I study the ground-up practices as responses. These responses are strategies of salvaging, refusal, defiance, and urban/global participation and intervention to address this crisis.

During various lunch sessions with Kevin Lim, I've had the pleasure of hearing about Studio SKLIM's research and building projects. It's wonderful spending time with someone who is so passionate about their work and is truly invested in making a difference in the world. A big congratulations to Studio SKLIM on the book! It will not only help others gain a better understanding of their work but also serve as inspiration to many.

Dr Woon Tien Wei
Co-founder, Post-Museum
Artist and Curator
Lecturer, LASALLE | University of the Arts Singapore

Introduction

by Kevin Lim

I established the eponymous studio in 2010 while living in Beijing, China. This coincided with the transformative period before and after the Olympics. The era of 2006–2011 saw big changes in the city. It showed the value of active evolution in architecture, and also signaled the need to respect traditional crafts and heritage buildings. This sparked my agency for effecting change in the built environment by the creation of this multidisciplinary studio.

Studio SKLIM integrates lessons from the past into its design process while embracing innovation and material research to expand its creative scope beyond contemporary architecture and interiors. This commitment reflects a dynamic and progressive ethos, tailored to adapt to evolving contexts while retaining a distinct sense of cultural identity.

The design process at our studio operates outside rigid methodological boundaries, embracing a framework that encourages comprehensive exploration and often exhaustive consideration of design options. Through collaboration with our clients, we foster dialogue to tailor solutions to each unique context. Leveraging both precise digital and intuitive physical models, we ease discussions to visualize and communicate our design intent.

Reflecting on our journey, as chronicled in this first monograph, we noticed repeating themes and obsessions in our projects. Central among these themes are the integration of structure, technology, technique, techne, materiality, and sustainability. These serve as the pillars of our creations and fuel our interactions with the local community.

Structural Dexterity through Rationality

At the core of our architectural approach lies a commitment to integrating structural principles into our designs. We explore the boundaries of structural design, often pushing conventional limits to achieve a heightened degree of flexibility in our spatial planning and architectural expressions.

In projects like the Hansha Reflection House, we employed innovative structural techniques to extend the possibilities of space. Here, we cantilevered the glued-laminated timber (glulam) floor beam 10 feet 5 inches (3.2 meters) to accommodate vehicular parking on a confined site and to provide an enhanced vantage point for the living and dining areas, offering picturesque views of the adjacent park.

Similarly, in the design of the +Pavilion, we employed a "nested" cross configuration of two glulam structural members to create a central "porous" structure with 16-foot (5-meter) cantilevers on the longitudinal sides. This not only resulted in a striking architectural element with minimum vertical structures but also facilitated the controlled flow of tropical rainwater through the roof's ruled surface geometry.

In the context of the Modern High School International project, our primary objective was to maximize space and natural light. To achieve this, we incorporated a series of post-tensioned beams along the longitudinal façade, eliminating the need for columns in the multipurpose hall and classrooms. This design decision not only enhanced spatial flexibility but also allowed for more communal discussion areas within the matrix of formal classrooms.

Evolving Techne and Revitalizing Craftsmanship

The synergy between technology, technique, and techne is central to the production and development of our projects. We embrace an array of production methods that marry modern innovations with traditional craftsmanship.

Our projects showcase a spectrum of approaches from both realms. Computer Numerical Control (CNC) routing breathes life into glulam timber and carbon steel, while terra-cotta undergoes transformation in wood-fueled kilns. Even the age-old practice of bending rattan experiences a revival, as heat and mechanical manipulation converge to produce new geometries. Double curvature concrete table panels take shape through membrane molds, enhancing the tactile experience of the space. Brickwork is reconfigured as bricklayers stack pieces incrementally to push projections. Prototyping is carried out using 3D prints as part of the design process before industrial heat-pressure molding of plant fiber biocomposites.

The integration of technology with craftsmanship fosters a harmonious relationship between the design process and artistry. Central to this approach is an ongoing dialogue with skilled artisans, whose expertise shapes and elevates our spatial creations. While it may sometimes require some encouragement for artisans to embrace new geometrical solutions and to depart from traditional mindsets, our interactions have yielded hybrid creations that are refreshing and yet rooted in tradition.

Material Relations

Our focus on materiality extends beyond mere structural and tactile considerations delving into the rich histories and cultural traditions embedded within them. During our work trips, we have found inspiration from materials used in the everyday lives of the places we visit: from observing traditional rattan furniture in Singapore and Malaysia, to savoring piping hot Marsala Chai in terra-cotta cups from roadside *chaiwalas* (tea sellers), and enjoying local snacks served on hand-pressed Sal leaf plates. As anthropologist Tim Ingold aptly notes, "To understand materials is to understand their histories—what they do and how they transform when manipulated—a process intrinsic to working with them."[1] This approach not only reveals cultural connections and reclaims memories, but also provides our work with linkage to the continuum of the past, present, and future.

In projects like Rattan Clouds, we draw inspiration from Southeast Asian chicken coops, infusing our modern display system with nuances of bygone eras. Meanwhile, terra-cotta forms the basis for the Terra-Cool building system in Lo-Hi Tech, capitalizing on its natural cooling properties to regulate ambient temperatures. In earthquake-prone Japan, our choice of glulam as the primary structural system for Hansha Reflection House reflects our commitment to seismic resilience, bridging traditional practices with modern engineering solutions.

Rather than viewing the past through a nostalgic lens, we approach it with curiosity, uncovering both mundane and ingenious aspects that remain relevant to contemporary life. This exploration leads us to re-evaluate "primitive materials" such as clay bricks, rattan, timber, terra-cotta, and plant fibers, for potential integration into our modern existence. Guided by a commitment to sustainability, we actively seek eco-friendly options, utilizing recycled and locally sourced materials, while exploring innovative and sustainable manufacturing practices.

---

1 Tim Ingold. "Toward an Ecology of Materials." *Annual Review of Anthropology 41*(2012): 434.

The creation of various building models is fundamental to the design processes employed by Studio SKLIM on each and every project.

Sustainable Futures

Sustainability now stands as a cornerstone of our design philosophy. In recent projects, we've embraced sustainability as a guide, drawing inspiration from the resourcefulness often found in less developed economies.

This journey has taught us valuable lessons in integrating low-cost sustainable design practices and strategies into the core of our architectural narratives. We see a deep link between sustainability and frugality. It makes us ask: "How can we do more with fewer resources?"

While we value technological advancements, we approach sustainability with caution, mindful of the potential pitfalls of overreliance on technology. Our preference leans toward passive methods that harness natural processes, incorporating more sustainable interventions as needed. An example of this was in Modern High School International. The project achieved "Platinum Standards" in their national green building certification system by having ample daylight strategies through large non-glare openings and skylights.

Sustainability isn't just a choice; it's an urgent imperative. As stewards of design responsibility, we are committed to shaping a future where sustainable practices are a necessity for the well-being of our greater community.

Creating Communities

Our selected portfolio showcased in this monograph encompasses a diverse range of projects, spanning from an intimate 301-square-foot (28-square-meter) interior to an expansive 86,111-square-foot (8,000-square-meter) building. These projects include both built and unbuilt works situated across a variety of cultural landscapes, including Singapore, Japan, South Korea, Thailand, and India. In each of these design journeys, we have tried to develop a cultural understanding of behavioral patterns as well as local practices to manifest our projects.

A significant milestone in our journey occurred at the close of 2023 with the completion of our largest architectural endeavor to date: an international school in Kolkata, India. Despite facing construction challenges stemming from the pandemic, our team—both off-site and on the ground—exhibited remarkable resilience and determination, overcoming many obstacles to bring the project to fruition. This achievement stands as a testament to the collective efforts and commitment of the collective teams. Another example where community involvement was pivotal to the project's success is the +Pavilion, where thirteen partners from both SMEs and MNCs joined hands in a bottom-up collaboration to advance the agenda for sustainable construction.

As our adaptation of the famous saying goes, "It takes a village to raise a building." Our experience reinforces this sentiment. Throughout our projects, we have collaborated with a diverse array of individuals and teams, ranging from individual artisans to large-scale construction crews. In this dynamic, we have taken on roles as both teachers and students. We foster a shared knowledge base that drives each project forward.

Next

Studio SKLIM is ready to embark on larger-scale projects to demonstrate our design philosophy beyond spatial aesthetics and refine programmatic aspects. We also wish to explore further with an integrated design approach that merges material innovation with sustainable practices. This holistic perspective underscores our belief that architecture should not only respond to immediate needs but also proactively contribute to the shaping of a sustainable future.

"Techne is a term that originated in ancient Greek philosophy and refers to a concept of craftsmanship. Techne emphasizes the manual dexterity, craftsmanship, and expertise required to produce something of value. It involves a combination of theoretical understanding, practical experience, and the ability to apply techniques to achieve desired outcomes."

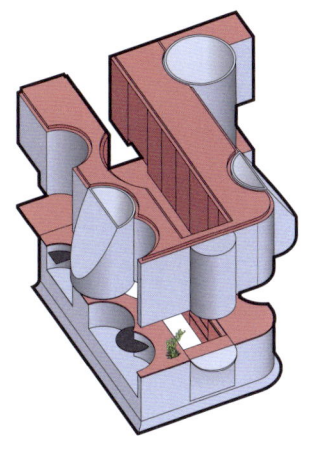

Voids Café

Food & Beverage
Singapore, 2019

"Voids are treated as form in this micro-café."

The table's base is made of a single concrete piece with curved profiles that allow customers to sit or interact closer, fostering better relationships.

The empty space in a coffee cup or matcha bowl was the form-giving inspiration for this micro-café spanning only 301 square feet (28 square meters). Negative spaces punctuate the space and circular geometries are consistently carried throughout the rest of the built form carving out seating booths, countertops, display shelves and overhanging canopies. It is a process of subtraction and addition to create the operational and anthropometrical needs of the café.

In this condensed space, it was essential that the numerous kitchen inventory was balanced with the customer zones, utilizing every nook to add to that experience. Several working and customer zones were created, including an experience/retail corner, a takeaway counter, seating booths, and even a small "Ritual Counter" for conducting workshops and making drip coffee or bowls of matcha (powdered Japanese green tea.)

1 Customer Service Zone
A Experience Circle/Display Cabinet
B Point of Sale
C Takeaway Counter

2 Kitchen Zone
D Food Preparation
E Coffee Station
F Coffee and Tea Rituals

3 Seating Zone
G Single Seating
H Couple Seating
I Standing Tables

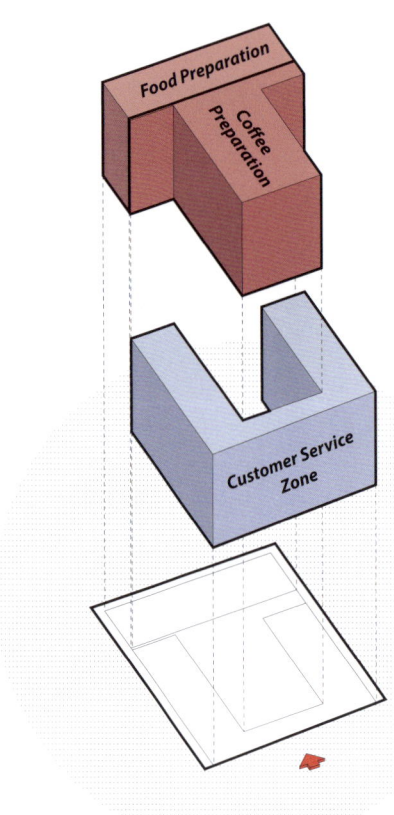
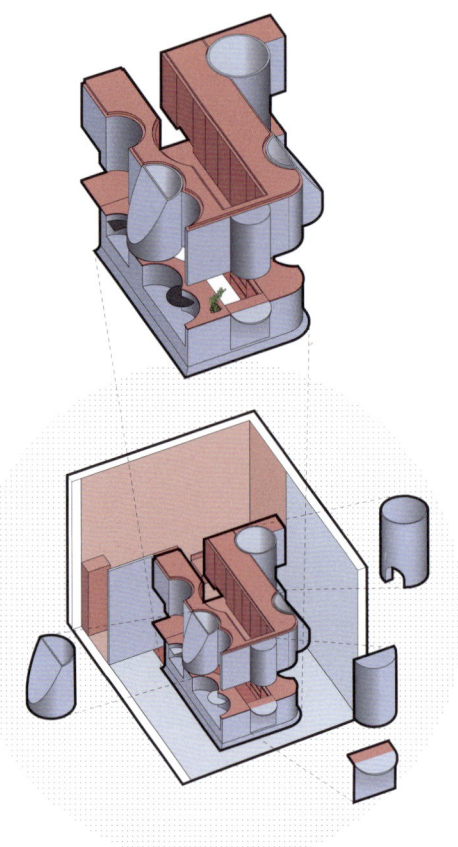
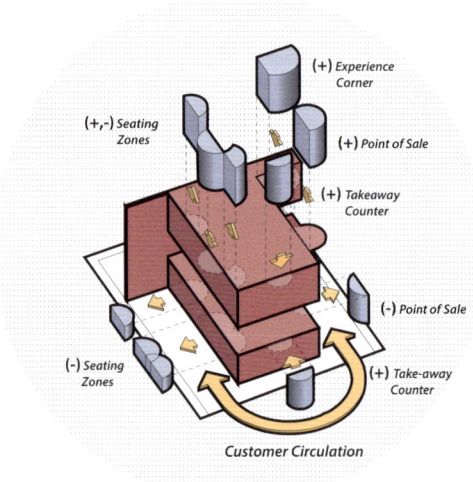

The experience circle was designed as a suspended enclosure where customers can duck under and experience the smell of different coffee grounds and tea products. Counter spaces were carved out to encourage a closer interaction between customer and barista, simultaneously bringing them in closer proximity to the coffee-making process with aroma and grinding/tapping sounds. Customer seating consists of circular cut-outs in the concrete counters, with matching petal-like tables to match.

Short sections

Voids Café

The tabletop is comprised of eleven custom pink concrete pieces, with the central piece featuring a gently bulbous profile that was created using a membrane formwork.

The main powdered pink concrete countertop was custom-cast in eleven separate pieces. Among these was a minimal surface concrete countertop for takeaways formed by using a special fabric formwork. Cracks were also purposefully cast in the concrete to allow planting to emerge from beneath, an inspiration taken from plants growing on old buildings. Circular metal tables were created to project from the walls and similarly from the concrete seating booths. The concrete counter block was visually made to be contiguous with the floor with adjoining gentle curved radii.

The entire volume was entirely holstered from the ceiling with no supports connecting the bottom countertop mass, giving a surreal lightness about the whole structure. The overhanging volume was also rendered in heavily textured stucco inspired from gritty coffee grounds to create an antigravity coffee cloud. The resultant aesthetic from subtractions and additions creates a massing that appears fluid with its own fuzzy logic, certainly not based on any premeditated form or symbol of what a café should be.

The textured stucco finish on the upper volume is inspired by gritty coffee grounds.

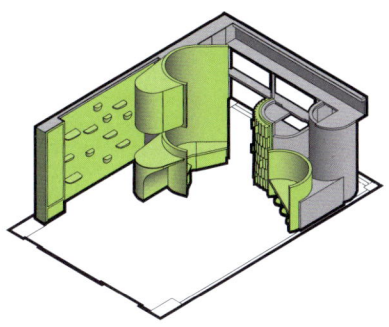

Deloitte Center for the Edge

Office
Singapore, 2020

"Nine agile work zones wrapped by plywood shells for a compact office."

The pendant lamp hanging over the meeting table was made of kenafcrete, which is a lightweight concrete derived from kenaf plant fibers.

The compact office may become increasingly ubiquitous due to the rising need to work from home in the post-pandemic world. For the Deloitte Center for the Edge (Asia-Pacific) office in Singapore, a multitude of working spaces were conceived to accommodate myriad working styles. The 344-square-foot (32-square-meter) office, located within the National Design Centre in Singapore, is designed with innate agility to transition from enclosures of individual concentration to collaborative spaces.

"We were looking for a 'third space,' one that extends the current spaces at Deloitte to have a different kind of conversation with clients and teams. We wanted a space that embodied the principles of 'provoke,' 'inspire,' and 'connect' in a real working environment that also showcased the future of work and working," said Duleesha Kulasooriya, Executive Director of the Deloitte Center for the Edge, who commissioned the space.

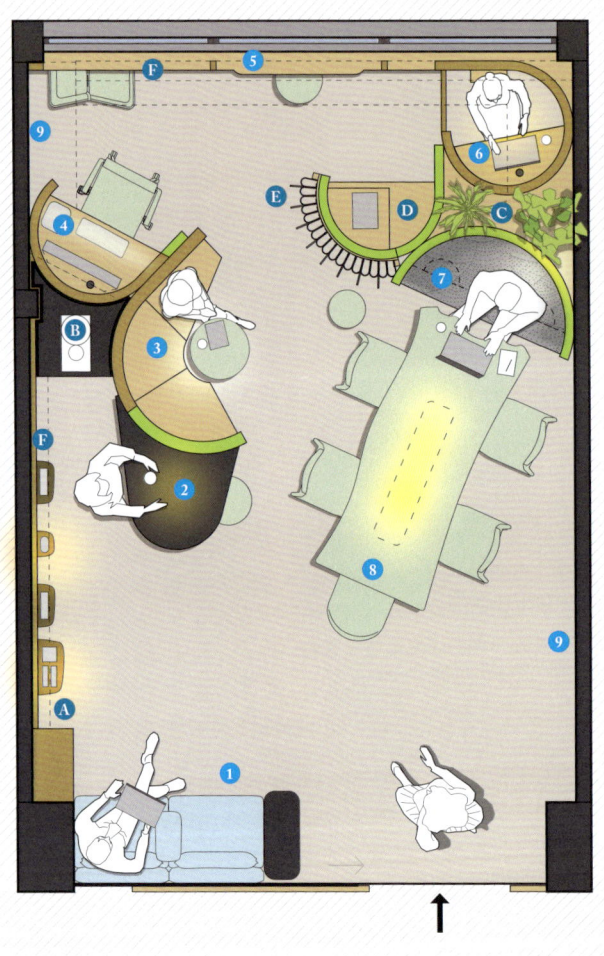

1	Soft Working	A	Artifact Wall
2	Octopus Bar	B	Pantry
3	Niche to Meet	C	Planter
4	Dedicated Workspace	D	Printing Station
5	Work with View	E	Felt Shelving Wall
6	Privacy Booth	F	Bottle Display Shelf
7	Work Platform		
8	Meet & Greet		
9	Think Wall		

Different anthropometrical work boundaries and patterns were studied to create nine distinct work zones:

1. Soft Working—Comfortable sofa work seating
2. Octopus Bar—Bar area within easy reach for work with a drink
3. Niche to Meet—Niche space for discussions between two to three people
4. Dedicated Workstation—Single full-height work cubicle
5. Work with View—Worktop with a view of the neighborhood
6. Privacy Booth—Fully felt-lined private booth with standing desk and seat

7. Work Platform—Concrete platform with more relaxed sitting options and docking niches for cork stools
8. Meet & Greet—Meeting table made from a local rain tree trunk
9. Think Wall—Collaborative wall with a dry-erase surface

Research and studies have shown that movement improves concentration. By offering different zones, movement is encouraged, and a variety of work zones can be used to suit different work requirements. The choice of curved surfaces is also supported by neurological research, making them more inviting and calming, allowing for more expansive conversations.

Interactivity among work colleagues is likely to be one of the primary incentives for a return to the office post-pandemic. The new office remains a hive for collaboration. The Think Wall is equipped with a dry-erase paint surface for brainstorming sessions and discussions. The Artifact Wall functions like a modern cabinet of curiosities where curated artifacts can provoke, inspire, and spark conversations.
A 100-bottle continuous display shelf provides their clients/collaborators with a dedicated area to keep their bottles in personalized containers (inspired by the Japanese bar system of *botorukīpu* ("bottle-keep.")

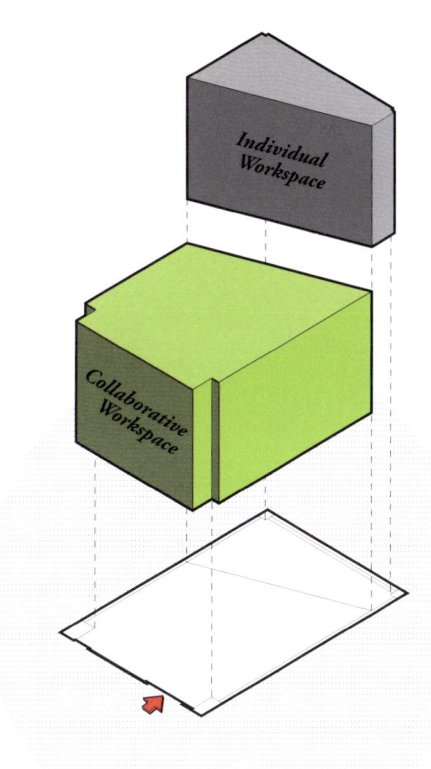
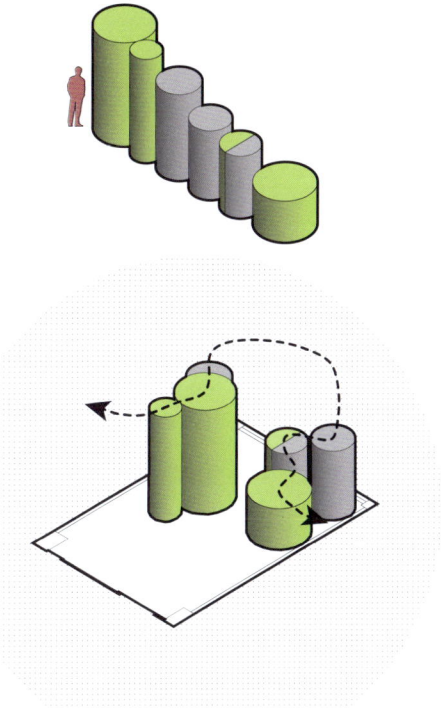
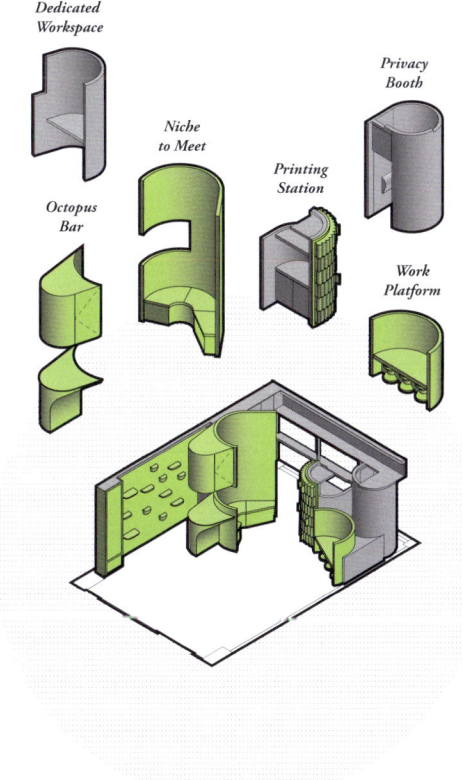

Felt pieces are secured with stationery clips to create pockets for slotting in pamphlets.

The nine work zones are strung together like jewels on a necklace, creating a continuous "loop of working spaces." The "loop" is further supported with six ancillary spaces, which include a Felt Shelving Wall for the client's research booklets and an Artifact Wall for an interchangeable display of showcase items. The geometry of these spaces was derived from experimenting with the client's research booklets, and this inspired the creation of curvilinear plywood shells to cuddle each work zone. The plywood shells vary in height according to sightlines and are oriented at different angles to create the perception of separate zones. The taller plywood shells increase privacy for the individual and act as health barriers between adjacent zones. Further cutouts facilitate visual interaction, and shells have been staggered to emit daylight and create visual depth.

Deloitte Center for the Edge

A plywood formwork was constructed as a negative shell to allow the pouring of concrete, thus forming the Work Platform.

The construction and selection of both carpentry and furniture have been geared toward sustainability and green practices. This was done by sourcing for eco-friendly materials/products such as vegan felt for felt shelving, local timber for a meeting table, Cork Family stools from Vitra and a custom-made pendant lamp from kenafcrete (kenaf plant fibers with lime binder). A dedicated area for potted plants also adds a biophilic touch to the office. The design and construction process has been kept honest and rudimentary to reveal the true nature of materials, such as curved layered plywood. Everyday stationery items, such as file binders and clips, were used to assemble the Felt Shelving Wall.

Construction during the pandemic lockdown was a challenge with national restrictions. This was overcome by using CNC-cut templates and utilizing differential cross-border lockdown situations to mitigate the fabrication process. These were transported a short distance across the border and assembled by a small team locally.

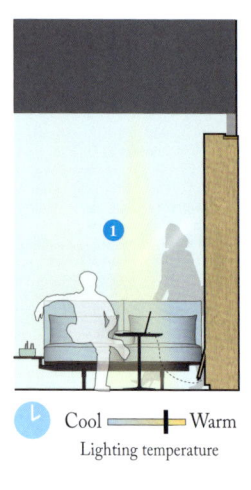
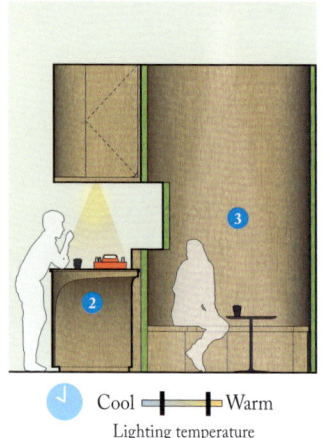
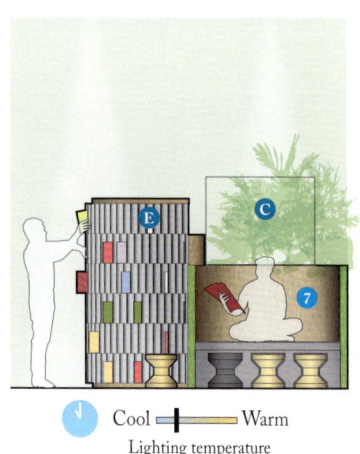

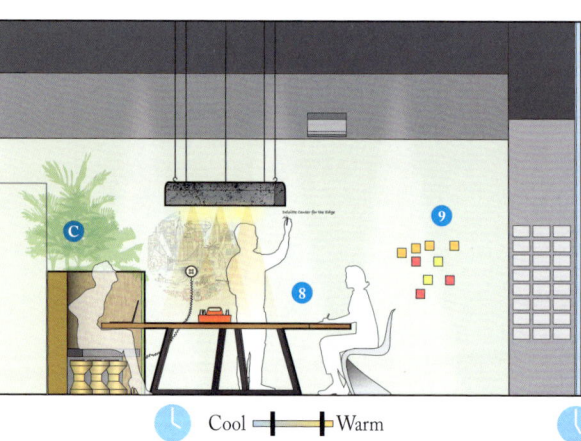
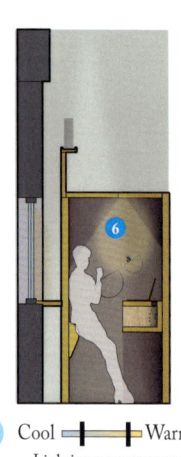
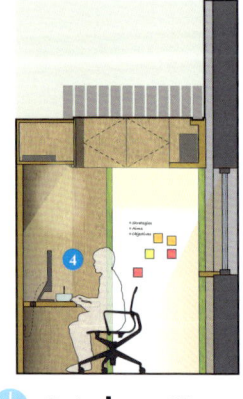
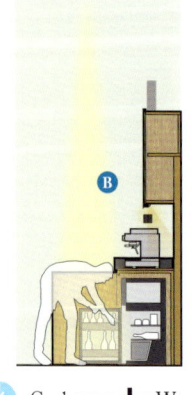

1 Soft Working	4 Dedicated Workspace	7 Work Platform	A Artifact Wall	D Printing Station
2 Octopus Bar	5 Work with View	8 Meet & Greet	B Pantry	E Felt Shelving Wall
3 Niche to Meet	6 Privacy Booth	9 Think Wall	C Planter	F Bottle Display Shelf

Lighting has been programmed with different color temperatures to subtly signal variable work/relax environments from the morning to the evening (for example, cool color temperatures gradually transitioning to warm color temperatures). Different work zones have been programmed with different light requirements.

"We were very impressed by what Studio SKLIM created that addressed the design brief exceptionally in a very small space," said Duleesha Kulasooriya. "In the short time we've been in the space, we've proven that it is a great space for expansive, creative dialogues, as well as collaborative work. We look forward to expanding its use to host small gatherings as we emerge from the pandemic."

The new office for Deloitte Center for the Edge challenges the new normal of the work environment with a wide range of work zones in a very modest footprint.

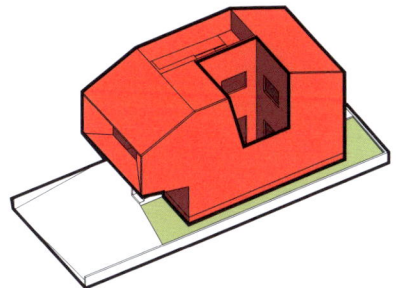

Hansha Reflection House

**Residence
Nagoya, Japan, 2011**

"Hansha Reflection House is a specific residence set to address the ephemeral moments of the surroundings with structural ingenuity and material sublimity."

The placement of load-bearing walls with continuous beams near the courtyard side was a strategic choice aimed at enhancing structural rigidity and minimizing eccentricity within the overall built form. These measures serve as effective solutions for limiting lateral movements during seismic events.

Situated at the entrance of Misakimizube Koen, a picturesque park along a lake, flanked by *sakura* (Japanese cherry blossom) trees, Hansha Reflection House was conceived as an integral part of its environment.

The house was organized into three distinct, programmatic zones of Public, Service, and Private, with further punctuation of the main massing with the landscape element, providing spaces for the courtyard and roof-deck. This base form was further chiseled with structure, daylight/ventilation, and viewpoint concerns.

   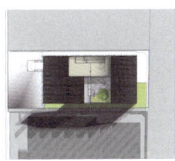

Site plan

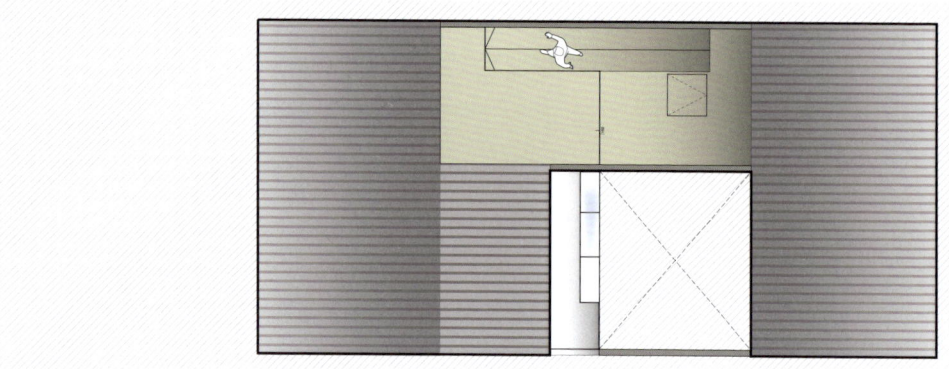

Roof floor plan

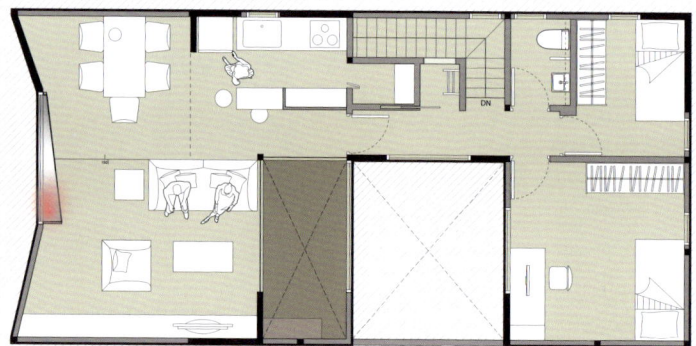

Second-floor plan

First-floor plan

Sixty-five percent of low-rise Japanese houses are constructed out of timber, a material that has the strongest weight-to-strength ratio among other building materials like concrete and steel. Using timber from a renewable source, coupled with a building technology that utilized a hybrid of traditional mortise and tenon joint system with steel bracketing, this house was able to push the ubiquitous "boxed" building envelope for timber residential construction in Japan.

Timber in the residence was sourced from renewable forests while a hybrid construction approach combined traditional mortise and tenon joints with steel bracketing.

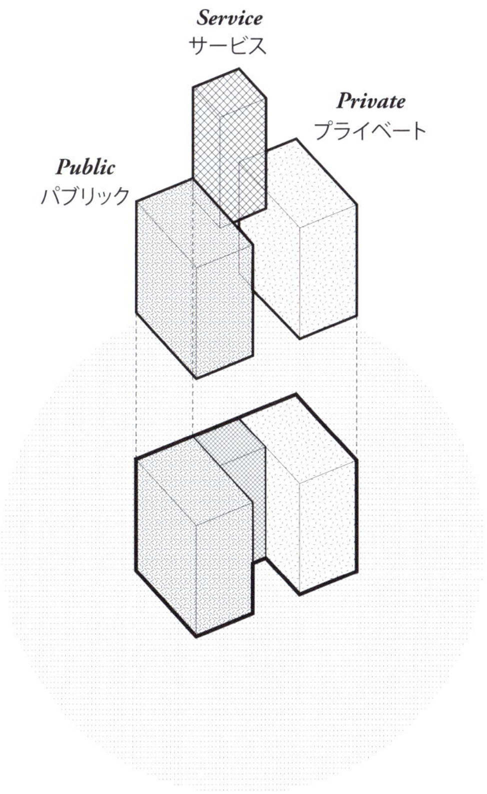

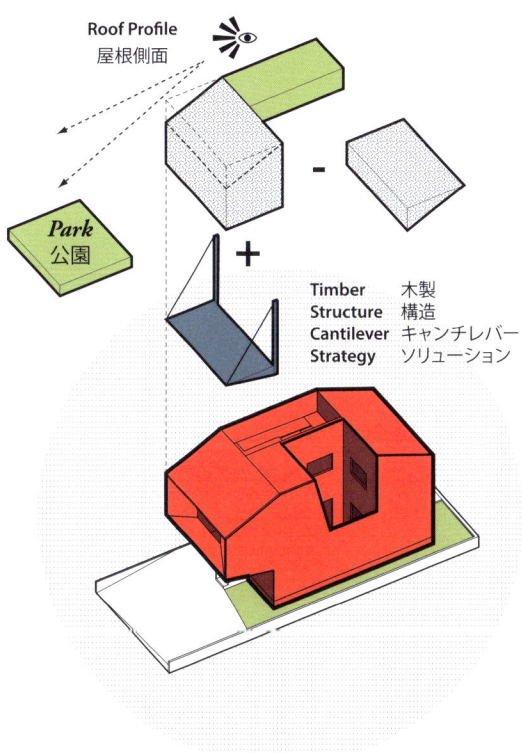

Hansha Reflection House

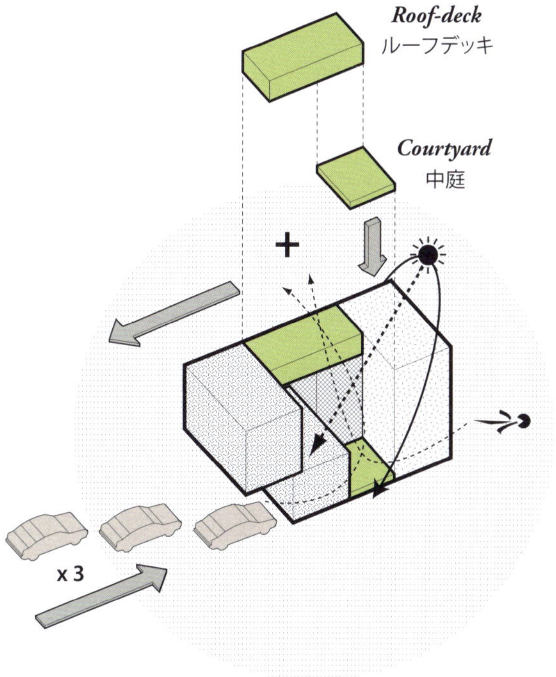

The decision to elevate the Public program to the upper level was driven by the need for parking space for three cars and the desire to capture scenic views of the park. The result is an impressive 11-foot (3.2-meter) wooden cantilever, a departure from the usual 5-foot (1.5-meter) norm. The initial structural concept evolved into a final solution inspired by bridge construction and bookshelf bracketing, with added structural reinforcement in the courtyard wall to minimize eccentricity and lateral movements during earthquakes.

The initial structural concept of employing a truss floor evolved into the ultimate structural solution, drawing elegant inspiration from bridge construction and the bracketing used in domestic bookshelves.

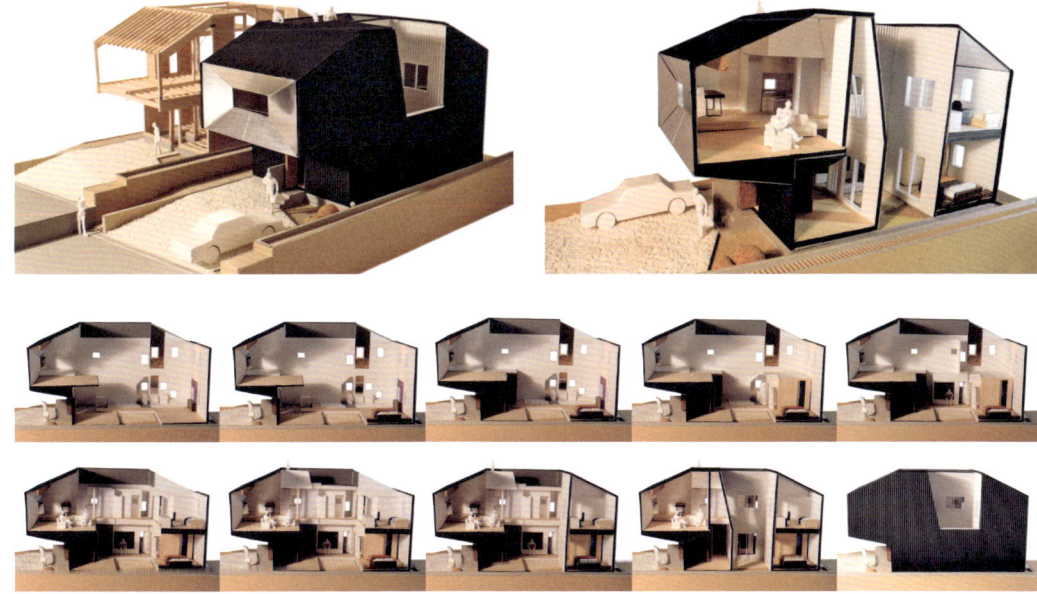

Hansha Reflection House

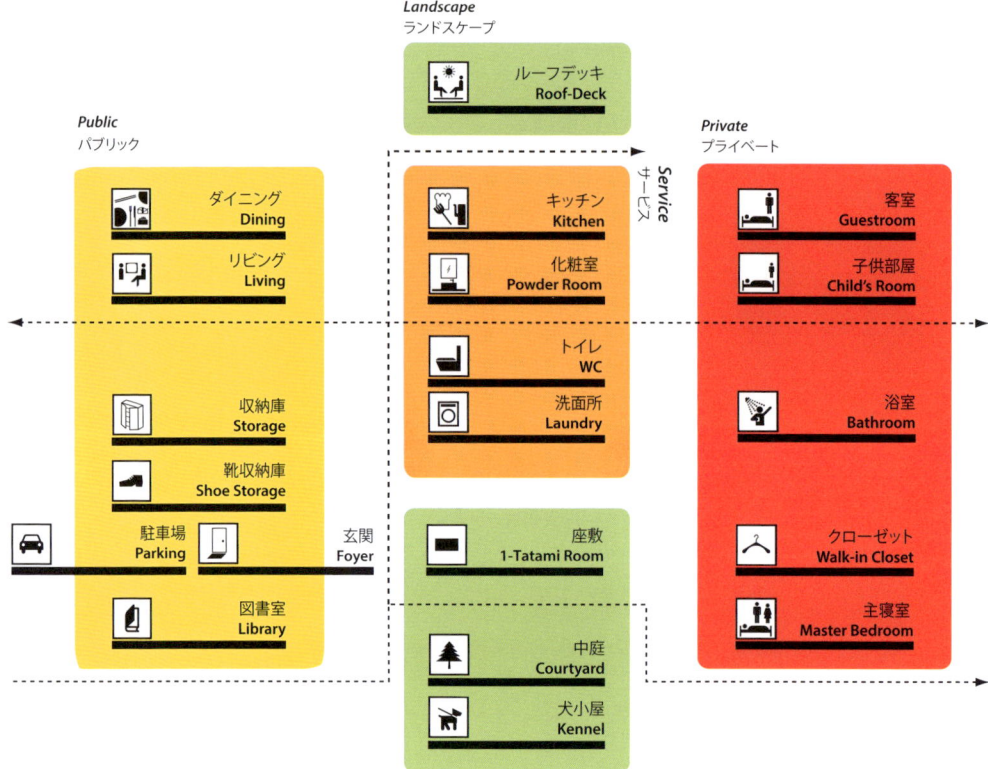

Organizational diagram

A *kamon* (family crest) light fixture was specially designed for the client to mark the entrance.

The exterior form of the building mirrors its inner structure, enabling the expression of inclined surfaces that respond to rainwater drainage and reflect the surrounding landscape. To bring the exterior *sakura* views into the dining area, an asymmetrical window ledge was thoughtfully designed, creating a seamless transition from outside to inside while framing the picturesque scenery.

The concept of "Reflection" takes on multiple meanings, encompassing the exterior reflection of the surroundings, the interior reflection of the environment, introspective reflection spaces, and reflection of the house's structure.

The landscape falls into three areas: the front yard, the courtyard, and the roof-deck. The front yard accommodates parking for three cars and becomes the entrance frame for the house. The connecting tissue to the park relies on the structurally evolved façade that visually associates with it and uses similar ground paving material.

The courtyard, an intimate private garden, forms part of the environmental funnel to dissipate hot air during summer. This space further anchors the master bedroom, a tatami introspective room, and a double-volume library. The roof-deck, the pinnacle of the house, further heightens one's sense of place with its surroundings and provides the perfect viewing platform for both *Hanami* (Sakura) and *Hanabi* (Fireworks) festivals.

Hansha Reflection House encapsulates the site's essence, creating a dwelling that looks back at its surroundings with a unique twist.

Hansha Reflection House

Rattan Clouds

**Retail/Office
Singapore, 2015**

"Rattan Clouds is a collection of modular rattan capsules configured for seating, storage, display, and lighting."

The rattan pieces are designed to be lightweight and portable enabling easy configuration by the user.

Inspired by the traditional Southeast Asian rattan receptacles, Rattan Clouds reinterprets rattan in new modern forms for a retail shop.

The ground floor unit, which has a lofty 15-foot (4.7-meter) ceiling space, is intended to serve as both a retail space and an office for Emporium of Modern Man—a shop that sells lifestyle goods for modern-day sensibilities. The shop's frontage is naturally prioritized for retail, and the office facilities are located further back, with access through a giant central pivot wall/door. The dividing partitions are minimal and light, consisting of white human-height wall/doors with storage cabinets and a floating concrete sales counter.

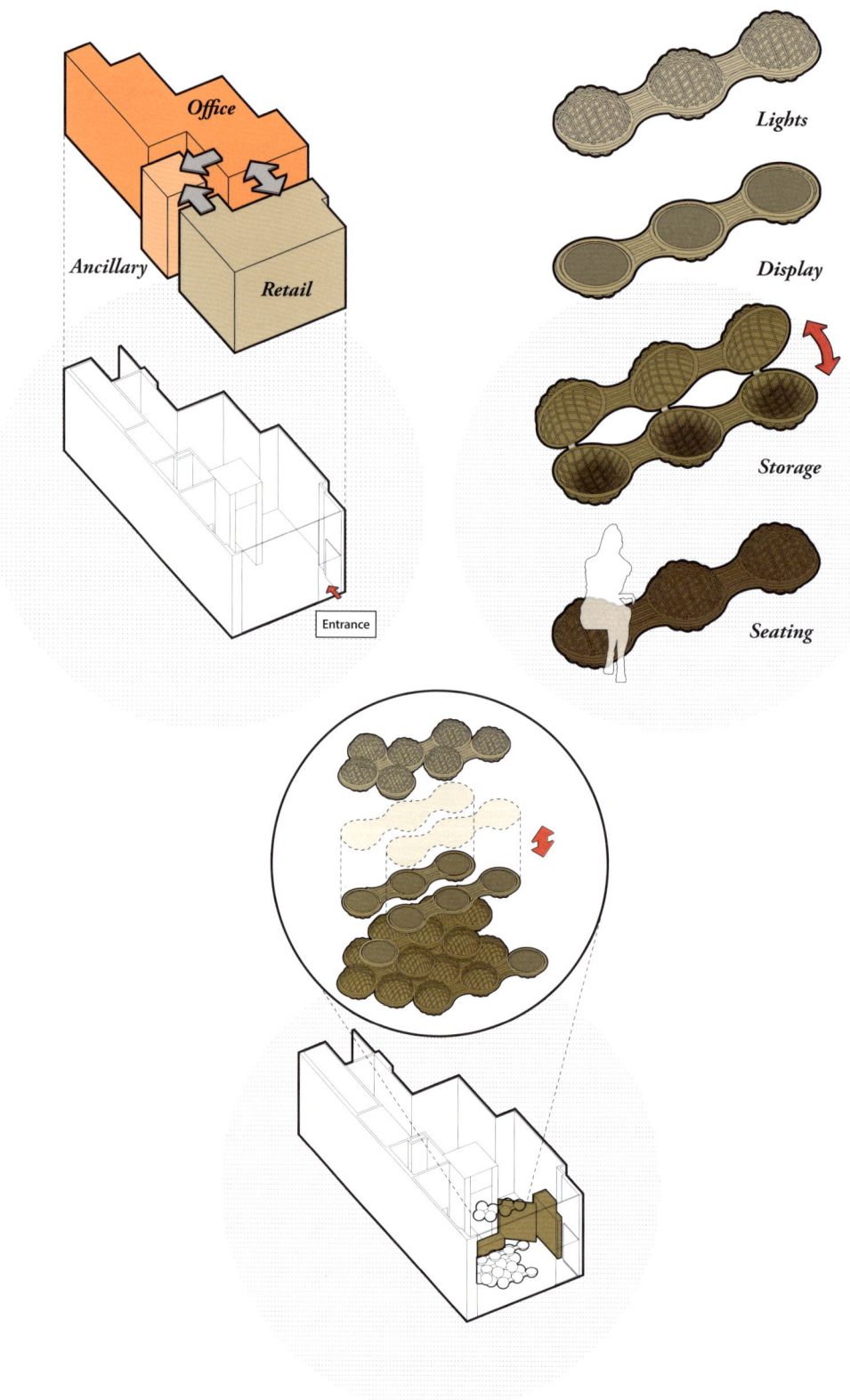

The retail space is designed to be nonpermanent, with flexible options to accommodate exhibitions, installations, and gatherings. Some of the Rattan Clouds capsules can be suspended from the high ceiling space and lowered/raised to accommodate different events.

Rattan Clouds was designed to meet the requirements of multi-configurability, functionality, and structural integrity, with traditional rattan craftsmen using existing techniques of bending rattan to different curvatures. The initial spherical concept of containing an object was developed to form two- or three-piece modules that could be stacked to create multilayered displays. Arched rattan also formed a strong base for seating. These Clouds were made operable to create a split level for storage and display.

The rattan pieces are handcrafted by artisans using a combination of heat, clamps, and nails to shape their curvatures.

Mechanical hand cranks enable the rattan modules to be raised and lowered, adjusting to the space requirements of the flexible area.

In the various permutations of the basic form, half-spheres of these modules were removed to form flat surfaces for display. These modules were held up by a system of brass pulleys and stainless-steel wires that could be lowered/raised by hand cranks. The last permutation of the module was to house halo-like illuminations that created shadow textures.

Rattan Clouds is a flexible, modular system that can shift according to the multiple uses of the space, adding a light and ephemeral touch to the retail experience.

Verdant Spine Office

**Office
Singapore, 2019**

"A verdant spine anchors the spatial organization of an office inspired by both natural landforms and vernacular forms/materials."

Custom-designed metal door handles were fabricated specifically for each door.

This new office for Cairnhill Law in Singapore offers a relaxed biophilic environment to a rather demanding profession. Taking cues from the overall branding strategy and name of the office, we adopted a natural palette of earthly accents and material tactility to complement the curvilinear "landforms." We were involved in the holistic design of the office from the interior design, furniture design to the various branding elements.

The spatial organization is anchored by a linear architectural datum that incorporates storage, shelving, printing station, an informal meeting niche, and an overhanging spine of flora. The aesthetic greenery draws inspiration from the tropical rainforest and was intentionally designed to be on the wild side, reflective of the flora in this region.

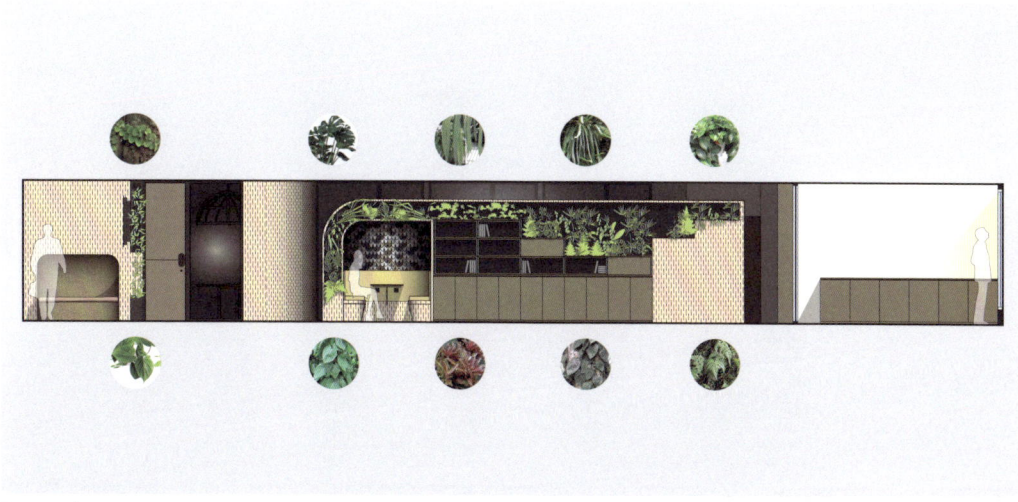

Longitudinal section

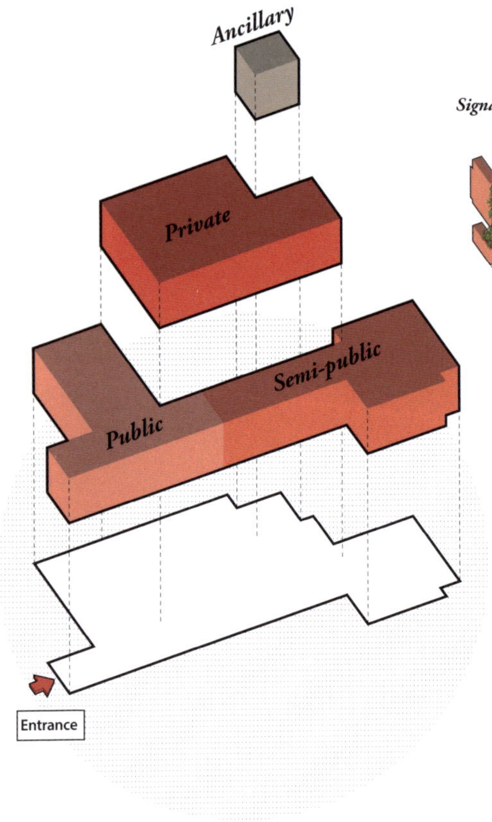

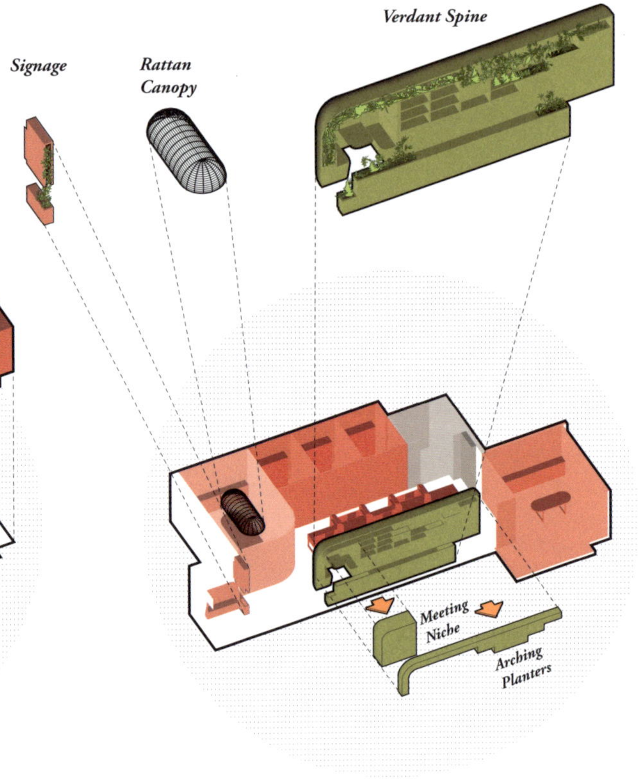

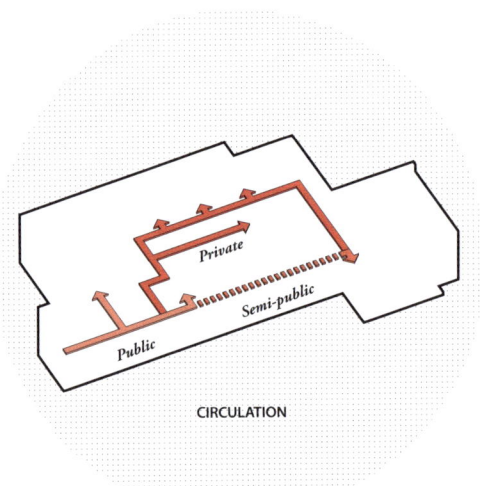

Pockets of planters were carved out from the carpentry and placed strategically to allow the vines to grow and connect through the dried lianas over time. This verdant spine also shields the private working cluster of the office from the more public circulation of their clients. Laser-cut felt pieces from leafy abstracts were custom fabricated to provide a softer acoustical cocoon for a meeting niche and cozy breakout area.

The curvilinear geometry of the partitions and carpentry are inspired by both natural landforms and vernacular architecture. The "landform" aspect of the design takes on a rough-textured stucco finish while the architectural components are addressed in the rattan canopy structure of the meeting room and mini-privacy canopies for the work cubicles.

Verdant Spine Office

1 Entrance Foyer
2 Meeting Room
3 Meeting Niche
4 Verdant Spine
5 Director's Room
6 Administration/
  Legal Assistant's
  Cubicles
7 Associate's Room
8 Printing Station
9 Pantry

The rattan light fixture measures 10 feet (3 meters) in length and has been skillfully handcrafted by craftsmen using traditional lashing methods.

The meeting room is an abstract of the vernacular communal longhouse. The overhanging 10-foot-long (3-meter-long) rattan canopy was designed in tandem with the meeting table to mirror each other in dimension. The contrast of the custom meeting table surface against the dark charcoal painterly walls adds to the overall atmosphere of being in a primitive hut. On a smaller scale, the work cubicles were designed to provide more visual privacy through partitions and rattan woven screens, configured to provide a balance between privacy and communication with the legal associates in their individual rooms. The utilization of local materials and geometrical nuances was purposefully designed with the spatial branding of the office in mind as regional professionals providing personalized legal services.

We believe in merging flora with the office environment to provide a balance between mentally demanding work and spaces that provide visual relief. The creation of this verdant spine manages the different workflows of the modern compact office by defining work zones and circulations while accommodating pockets of wild nature. We silently hope the plants will eventually take over the pockets and spread on the surfaces they now inhabit.

The 450 pieces of acoustic felt in the meeting niche were installed by hand.

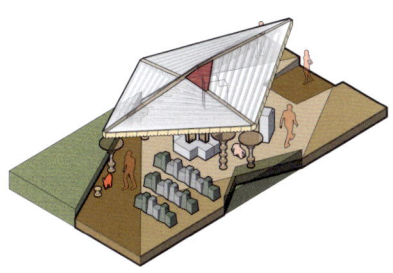

+Pavilion

**Pavilion
Singapore, 2022**

"The Swiss cross inspires the structural concept of a glued-laminated timber pavilion showcasing a vignette of a sustainable built environment."

The primary "nested" structural members of the pavilion are assembled using "glued-in" rod connections.

The +Pavilion serves as a poignant reminder of the pressing need to reduce the carbon footprint within the built environment—a critical component of Singapore's Green Plan 2030. It underscores the ways in which industry players can contribute to this crucial effort.

Globally, the built environment collectively accounts for a staggering 39 percent of carbon emissions, of which 11 percent is embodied carbon and the remaining 28 percent is from building operations. Embodied carbon encompasses emissions released during the manufacturing, transportation, and construction phases of a building. Remarkably, 11 percent of global carbon emissions are irrevocable once buildings are constructed. Therefore, it is imperative to prioritize sustainability and circular design principles from the inception of building design and construction processes to effectively mitigate the carbon footprint of the built environment.

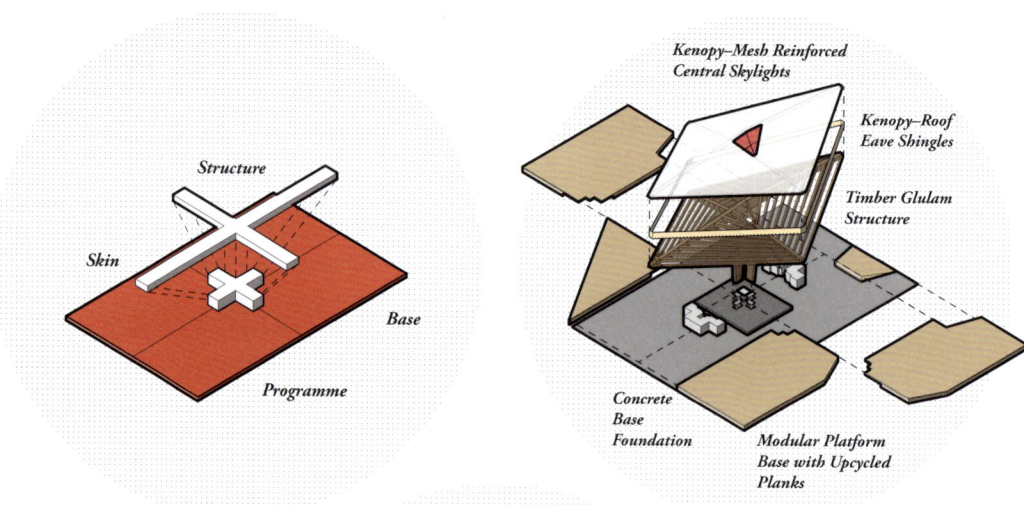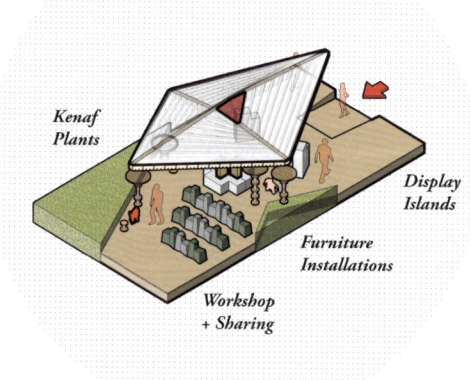

Designing sustainable buildings necessitates more efficient construction methods and a heightened focus on the reusability and durability of buildings and building materials. +Pavilion is based on a modular design and construction with prefabricated, pre-assembled modules, and "fit-for-purpose" services.

The architectural and structural design of +Pavilion draws inspiration from the Swiss cross. Two sets of tapering columns and purlin members, originating from this geometry, form the 16-foot (5-meter) cantilevering supports for the roof. The primary structure is constructed from Swiss glued-laminated timber (glulam), fabricated using a 5-axis CNC machine, enabling the production of subtly rotational curved roof rafters. The single module within this pavilion is just one element of a geometric tessellation.

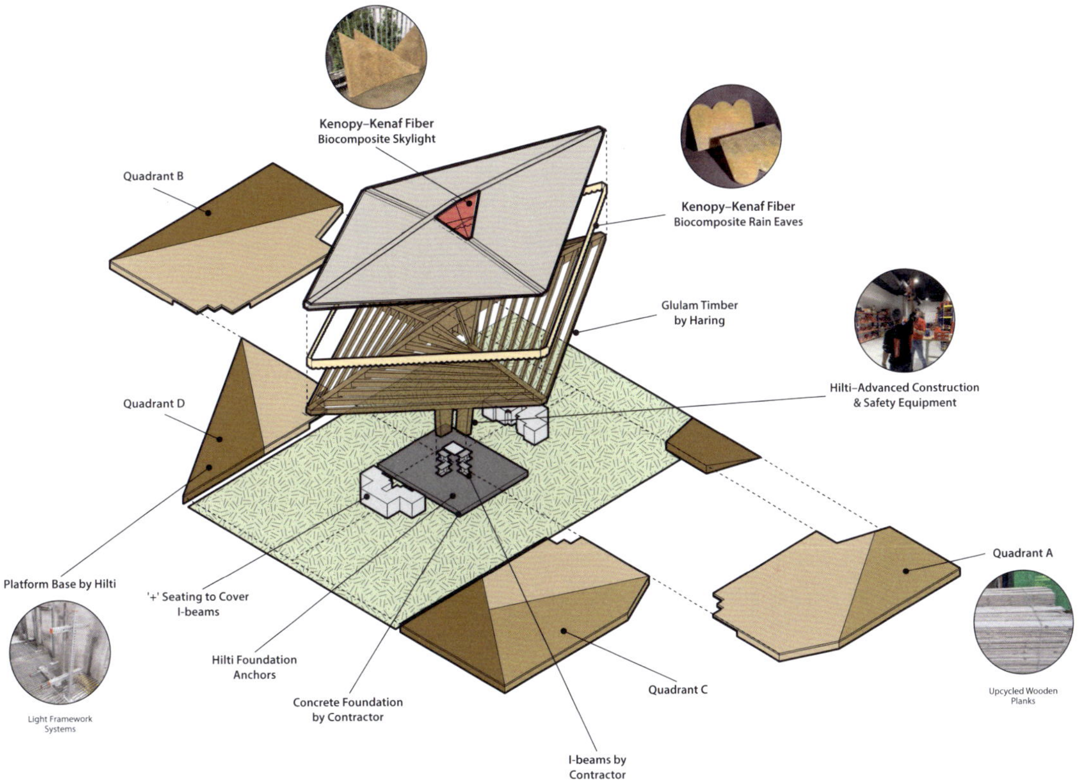

Exploded construction view

The structural rafters are milled using a 5-axis CNC machine, resulting in members with rotational curvatures.

Two sets of triangulations converge in a diamond configuration, creating a 120-degree angle at the pair of lower, opposite roof ends. This configuration allows three modules to combine into a substantial shelter and extend indefinitely into a woven shelter tapestry.

The glulam structure is counterbalanced by prefabricated reinforced concrete panels, connected through innovative anchoring and glued-in rod connections. The floor expands into a platform with a modular off-site bolt-and-nut system, reducing energy-intensive welding work. This modularity offers design flexibility for various engineered structures, and pre-fabrication ensures precise manufacturing unaffected by weather conditions. Both factors contribute to standardized and efficient assembly, resulting in overall cost savings in building construction.

The bolted modular supports significantly reduce carbon steel usage, facilitating carbon footprint reduction and enabling reuse for future modifications. The floor base incorporates timber composite floor panels upcycled from a previous project, where they previously served their first life cycle already.

Additional materials include innovative biocomposites made from the kenaf plant for roofing components, such as reinforced central skylights and rain eaves. Notably, this marks the first exploration of Kenaf Fiber Biocomposites as roofing material in Singapore. The boards utilized for exhibition signage are crafted from recycled coffee grounds.

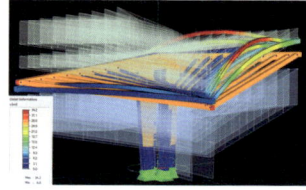

Finite Element Analysis (FEA) structural model, showcasing global deformation in one of the structural load cases.

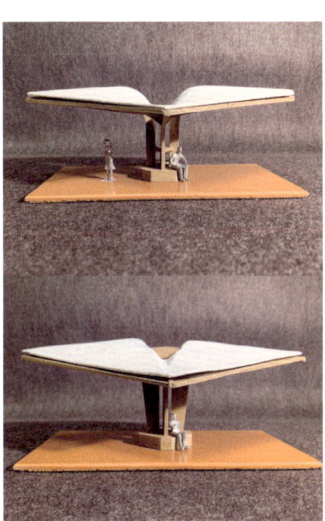

+Pavilion

Showcase of sustainability–
Kenafcrete and Kenaf Fiber
Biocomposite samples

+Pavilion is designed not only to attract attention but also to encourage engagement among visitors. The furniture within the pavilion, apart from providing seating and spaces for interaction, serves as a showcase of sustainability, featuring natural and recycled materials. Cork and rattan furniture highlight the use of natural materials, while recycled polypropylene, derived from a mixture of recycled household waste, demonstrates the possibilities of recycling.

The +Pavilion program at Marina Barrage includes multiple workshops and gatherings to foster discussions on sustainable building design and construction. Complementary exhibition signage provides in-depth insights into the pavilion's story and offers educational content on sustainability.

+Pavilion embodies the "sum of parts" approach required to combat climate change holistically: starting small, collaborating as an ecosystem, and working together to transform ideas into reality. This project marks the inception of a larger vision, symbolizing our commitment to revolutionizing the way we build.

The pavilion was relocated to EHL campus, Singapore for its second life cycle.

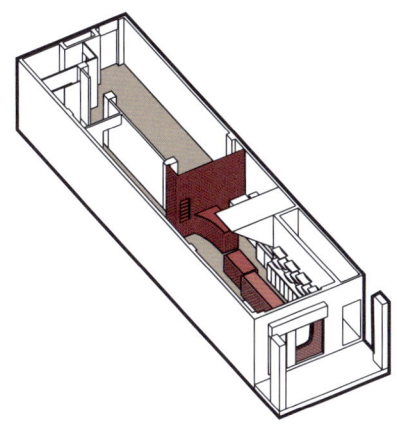

Brick Bakery

Food & Beverage
Singapore, 2014

"Brick is pushed to its boundaries as a building block and brand identity for an artisanal bakery."

The menu board is constructed using the underlying geometry of the stairs that lead to the upper floor. The menu itself is crafted from timber pieces suspended by hooks on a pegboard.

Nestled in the heart of the former red-light quarters of Keong Saik Road, Singapore, and among gentrified shophouses, resides an artisanal bakery.

Taking branding cues from the bakery's name, brick was chosen as the ubiquitous material to construct most of the spatial concepts. Bricks are predominantly used as architectural building blocks. In this instance, the material configures itself to form both exterior/interior, structural/nonstructural elements in the form of frontage, countertops, ventilation holes, furniture, partitions, and floor. The limits of the material are tested with both linear and double curvature geometries, construction joints, and tiling patterns.

1 Seating
2 Bakery Display
3 Cashier/Control Station
4 Coffee Station
5 Bar Seating
6 Storage
7 Kitchen
8 Restroom
9 Wash Area

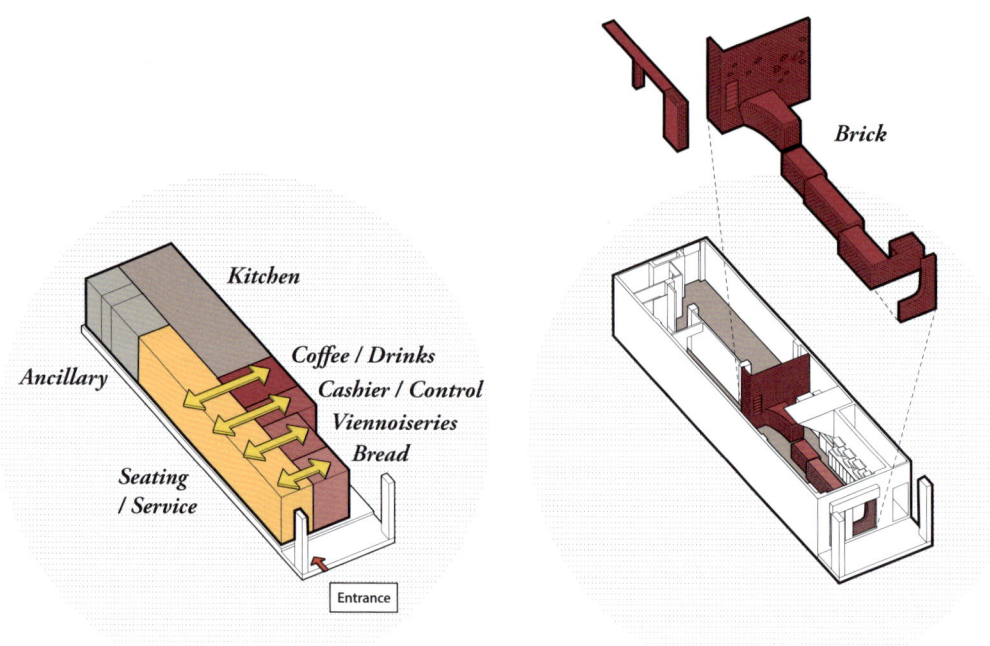

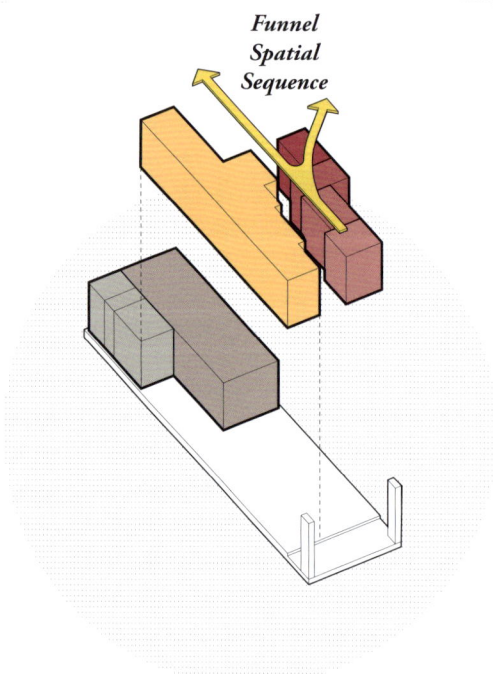

Brick Bakery

Programmatically, the functions of seating, display, service, kitchen, and back of house are distinctly lined up in a linear configuration due to the nature of the shophouse. The spatial sequence upon entry is almost funnel-like and slowly opens up to a fully fledged brick wall with a geometrically challenging coffee station. Each brick counter block houses a distinct function (Bread, Viennoiseries, Cashier/Control Centre, and Coffee Station), and is staggered to permit more standing space and interaction with the baked products. Bricks are strategically removed from the dividing kitchen wall to permit both aromas from and visual sightlines to the inner workings of the kitchen.

Custom canvas "bread hammocks" and linen containers were created as flexible display shelving for the freshly baked bread.

To permit a greater flexibility in the arrangement of bread displays, pegboard was used to line an entire wall. Custom canvas shelves were also designed as miniature hammocks to display the bread in linen bags, creating a softer and playful contrast to the hard-edged brick modules. In reference to the character of the shophouse, the underside of the wooden stairs was intentionally expressed and reinterpreted as the menu board for the bakery.

The craft in artisanal bakery was taken as a reference for the details in the shop, which included a variety of brick-tiling methods and also is reflected in the choice of custom furniture. The freestanding tables and stools take reference from the traditional craft of constructing furniture with mortise and tendon joints, further adding to the atmosphere and detail synonymous with the craft of baking.

The furniture was crafted by local carpenters using a traditional, nailless system of mortise and tenon joints.

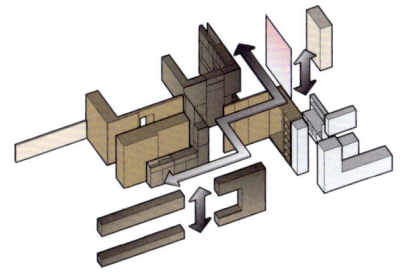

Ombré Patchwork Apartment

Residence
Singapore, 2017

"Ombré timber tones have been patchworked onto timber panels, gradually transitioning the space toward increasing privacy and warmth."

The apartment, located in the heart of the residential Cairnhill district of Singapore, is home to a working professional couple and their young son. The design brief called for an environmentally friendly home that resonates well with feng shui principles.

The material selection and construction methodology were carefully researched and executed to favor prefabrication and off-site finishing. Ecologically friendly materials, or materials that meet local green standards, were sourced, alongside materials that emit low VOCs (Volatile Organic Compounds). These include the natural oiled timber floorboards for the bedrooms, the prefinished timber veneer, plywood for carpentry, and the paints used.

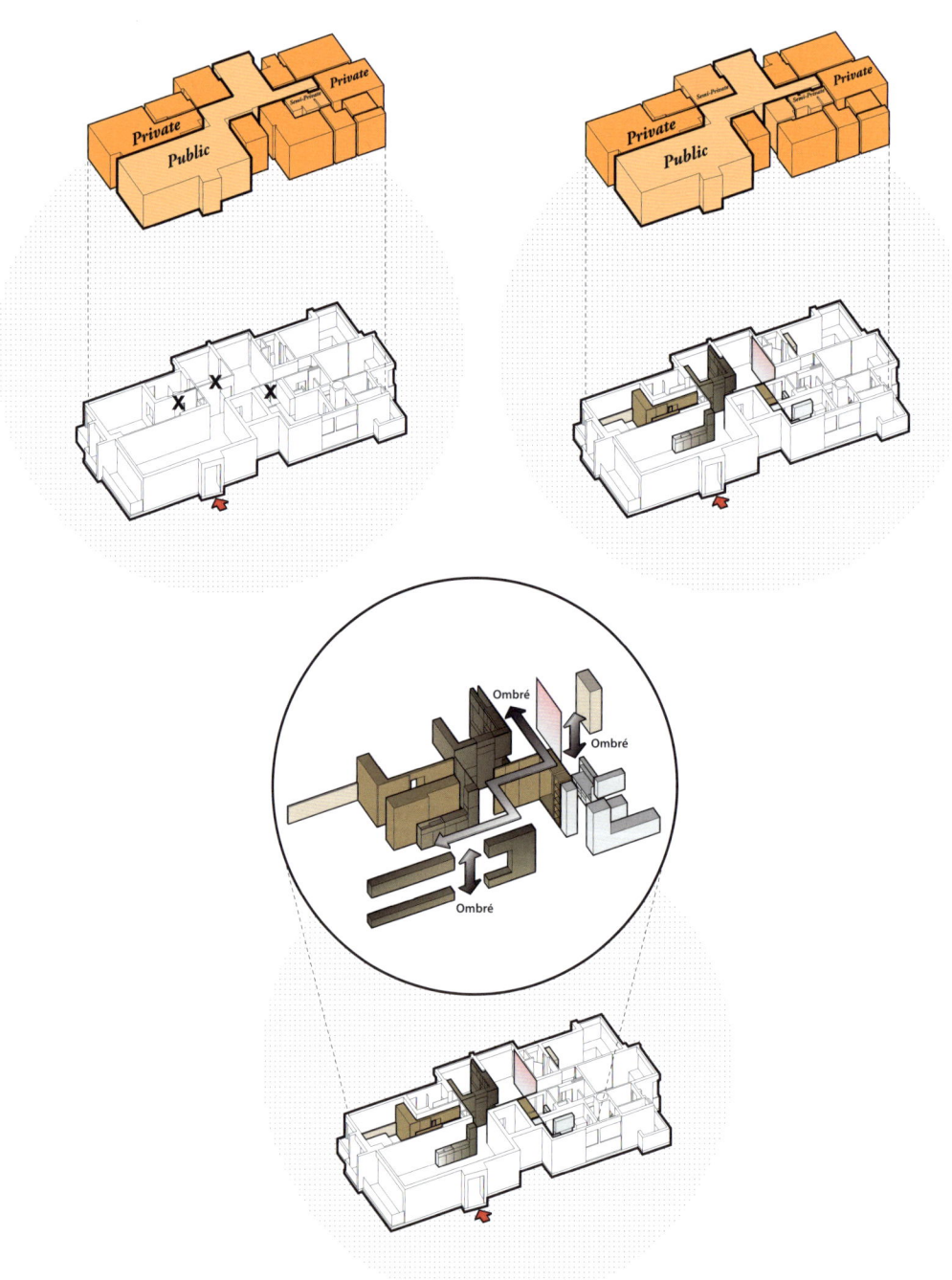

Upon entry into the apartment, visitors are greeted by cabinets of three timber tones that transition vertically from the charcoal black Italian tiled floor to the graded timber tones. The cabinets alongside the entrance are lightened gradually toward the top, while the other facing cabinets are gradually darkened in a horizontal patchwork fashion. The intention is to create a transitional path that guides from a more public space to a more intimate setting, hence from lighter to darker tones. The ombré effect is migrated to the dining room wall with a spray-painted finish from gray to pink-toned gradients.

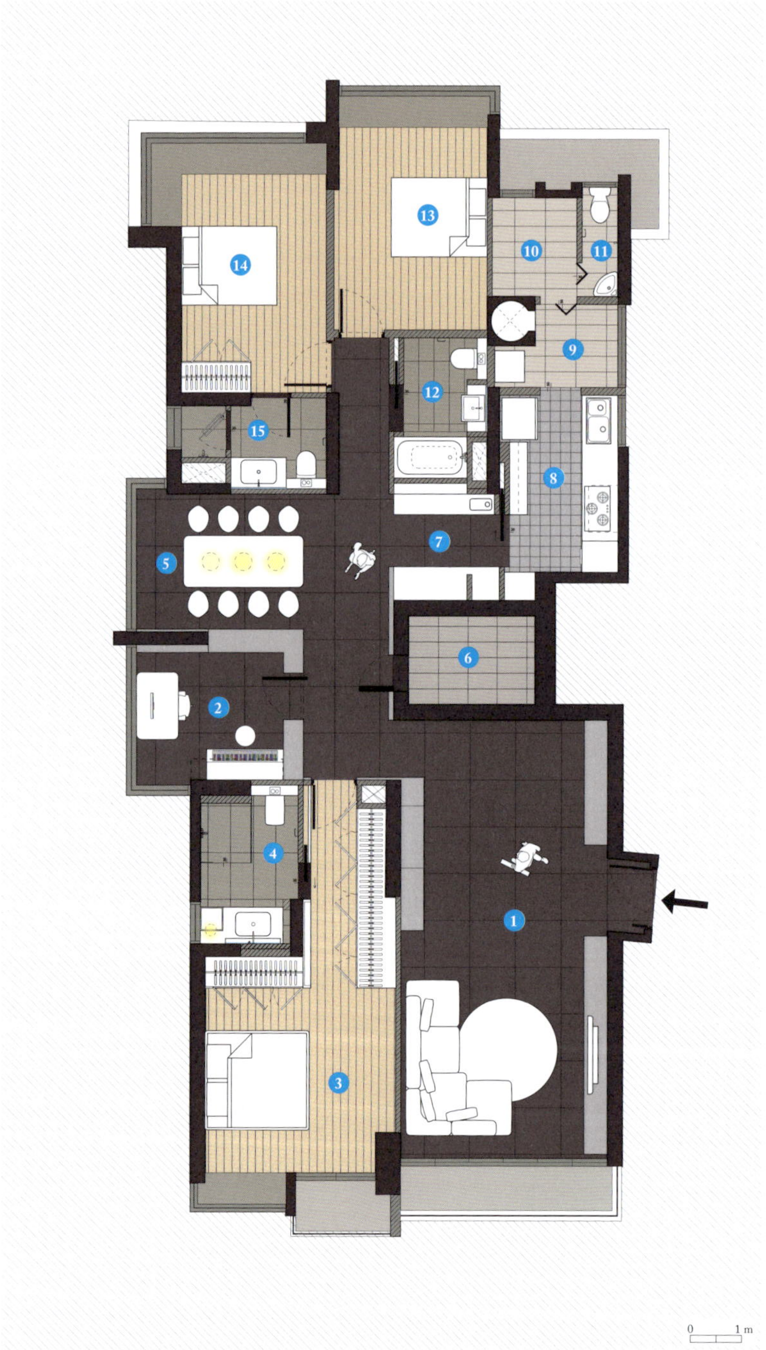

1 Living Room	6 Storage	11 WC
2 Study	7 Dry Kitchen	12 Powder Room
3 Master Bedroom	8 Kitchen	13 Playroom
4 Master Bathroom	9 Yard	14 Junior Master Bedroom
5 Dining Room	10 Maid's Room	15 Junior Master Bathroom

The wall adjacent to the dining room is painted in a gradual transition of colors ranging from gray to pink.

The dining room is a rather playful but intimate space. An 8-foot-long (2.4-meter-long) marble top table with a copper frame anchors the space. This was specially customized and designed by the studio to match the overhead pendant lights and the adjoining preparation area. The juxtaposition of the masculine character of the study and the more feminine dining area creates a dialogue of opposites, balancing the atmosphere in a complementary way.

The existing room next to the dining area was demolished and transformed into a semi-porous study with visual connectivity to the adjoining spaces. The use of black textured sheet metal with dark tones of timber gives an industrial but intimate presence to the study, much suited to the working habits of the husband.

The dry kitchen area was conceived to serve as an intermediary zone between the formal kitchen and the dining room, where food could be garnished and placed. This area also serves as the baking preparation counter for the wife. Complementary tones of navy blue with brushed gold handles add some bling to the large, veined marble top and solid bamboo composite shelves (recycled offcuts).

The entrance to the kitchen is guarded by custom industrial sliding doors that open up to a monochromatic row of aluminum kitchen cabinets. The only hint of playfulness carried from the dining room are the random patterned floor tiles.

While black tiles demarcate all of the public zones, natural-oiled oak floorboards were used in the bedrooms to transition toward a more private and warmer realm. The master bedroom door is hidden and flush with the timber patchwork wall, and opens to a walnut veneered flanked volume, which houses the wardrobes. This volume also leads to the master bathroom. A color palette of predominantly dark brown, black, and white was chosen for the bathroom, with luxurious rose gold and yellow gold accents providing a touch a old-fashioned glamour.

The Ombré Patchwork Apartment strings together spaces that are unique to each individual user and blends them cohesively through this modern timber patchwork.

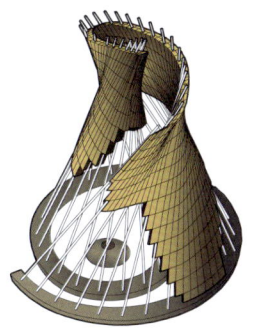

Bamboo Umbrella Pavilions

Pavilion
Bangkok, Thailand, 2018

"Bamboo pavilions inspired by Thai umbrellas provide sustainable shelters for an adventure park."

A set of four pavilions are sited near the entrance compound of a triathlon adventure park in Bangkok, Thailand to provide shelter for the park's activities. These pavilions house different programs: central stage, toilets, washing facilities for bicycles, drink stations, light refreshments area, lounge, exhibition area, recuperation areas and a tower for moon gazing.

The form and structure were derived after studying Thai bamboo umbrellas with their center-heavy structure and lighter, cantilevered ribs. The central supporting structures of the pavilion with their structural redundancy could additionally incorporate a rainwater collection and filtering system for the park. These central water catchment towers use a stone filter where varying granules of stones are layered in steel cages like gabions to remove impurities. The filtered water could be used for the washing mud from bicycles, the general cleaning of pavements, and watering of landscape.

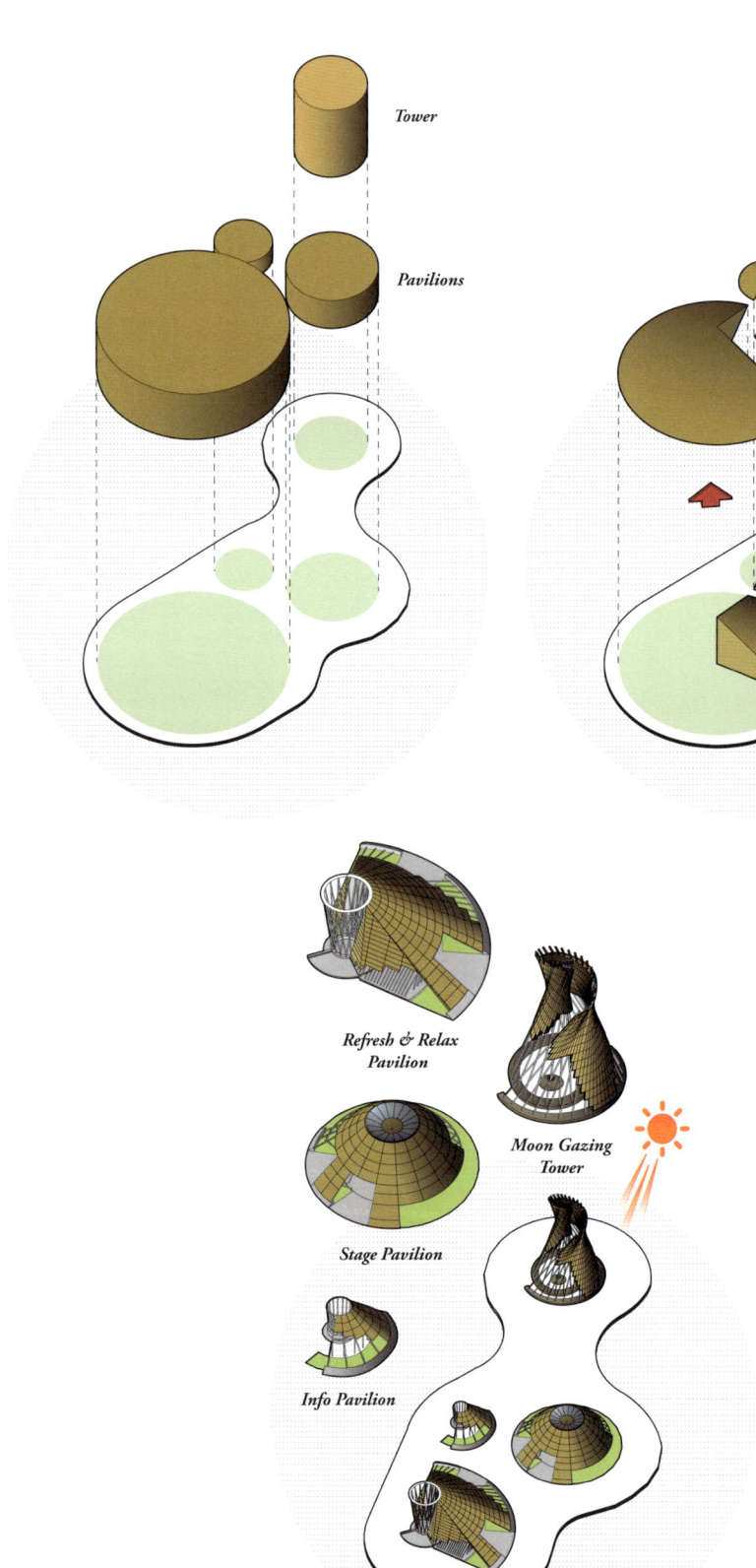

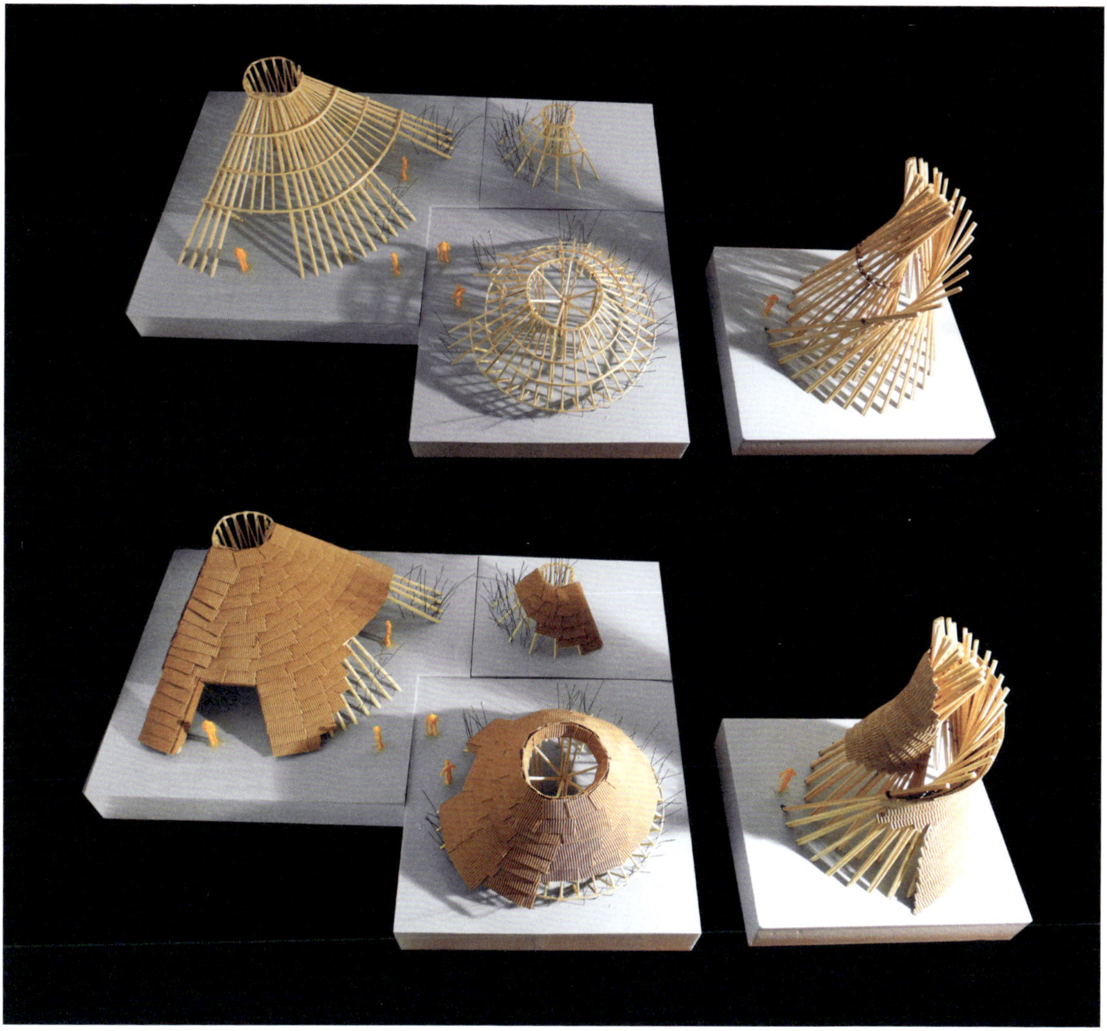

Solar radiance and roof geometry studies of Moon Gazing Tower

The different sizes and heights of the pavilions vary according to their programmatic functions and shelter requirements. Solar radiation maps throughout the year were studied to determine the optimal positions for the bamboo shingles. Additional landscape planting was incorporated to provide shade and privacy.

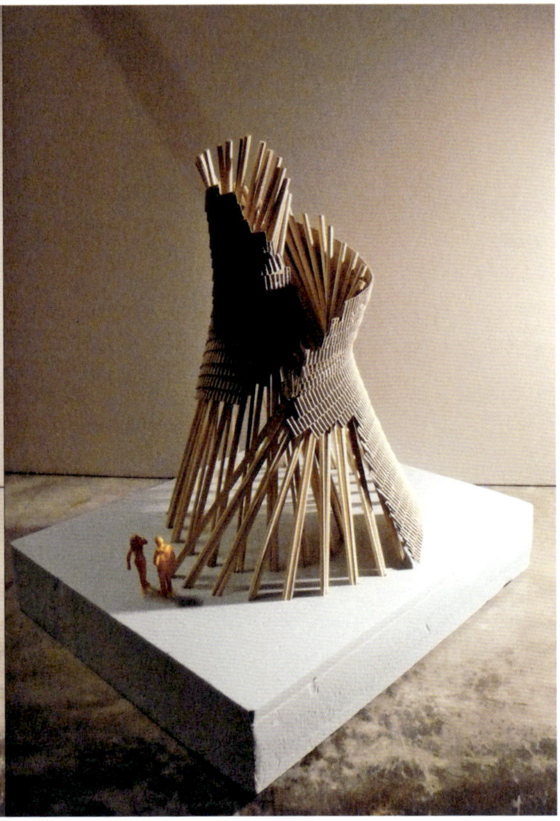

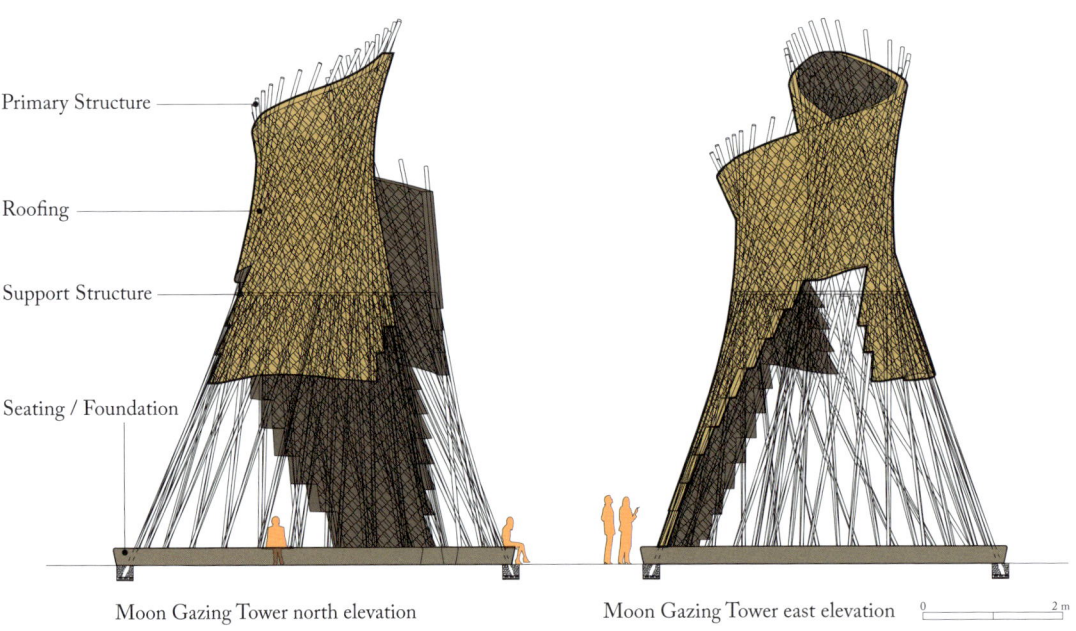

Moon Gazing Tower north elevation

Moon Gazing Tower east elevation

- Primary Structure
- Roofing
- Support Structure
- Seating / Foundation

0   2 m

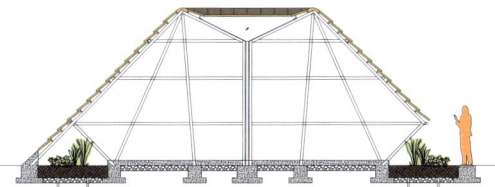
Medium Pavilion typical section

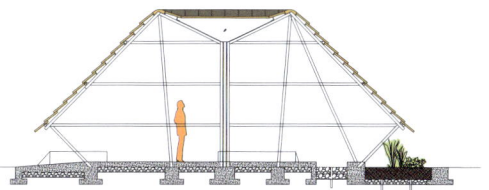
Medium Pavilion entrance section

Small Pavilion section

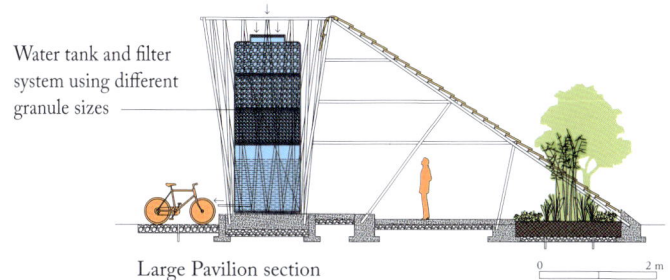
Large Pavilion section

Water tank and filter system using different granule sizes

The Moon Gazing Tower follows a different structural configuration and utilizes the physics of reciprocal structures to maintain its integrity. Visitors enter the enclosure through an opening in the spiral plan that slowly leads to the vortex of the structure, which also frames the moonlit sky. Seating is provided alongside the raised concrete foundation. This moon-gazing pavilion provides a natural organic enclosure for contemplation and the metaphysics of being one with nature.

The collection of Bamboo Umbrella Pavilions provides rudimentary shelter for sports programs, and also facilitates a contemplative venue for visitors to the park.

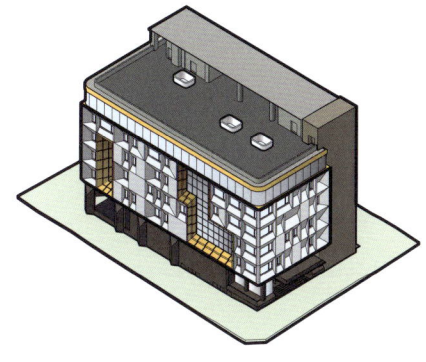

Modern High School International

Education
Kolkata, India, 2023

"A series of strategic voids punctuate a rectangular building mass and carve out pockets to emit natural daylight into the learning commons of an urban school."

To pave the way for construction on site, a *Bhumi Pujan* ceremony was conducted by Brahmin priests. Rooted in *Vastu Shastra*, this ritual holds significance in inviting divine blessings and fostering positive energies before the commencement of construction.

In Kolkata, India, the existing basketball courts of Modern High School for Girls have been transformed into a six-story co-ed international school. Situated at a noisy and congested traffic intersection, the building's massing begins as a rectangular block with north–south long elevations and east–west short elevations.

The choice of a north–south longitudinal orientation with east–west as the short frontage aims to maximize natural daylight in south-facing classrooms year-round and provides an elevated panoramic view of a recreational lawn and the broader cityscape of Kolkata. This alignment also exposes a large façade surface to the prevailing wind, unobstructed by nearby infrastructure.

The International Baccalaureate (IB) curriculum brings about a shift in teaching pedagogies, leading to a reorganization of spatial layouts. Students now move to resource centers instead of remaining stationary in classrooms.

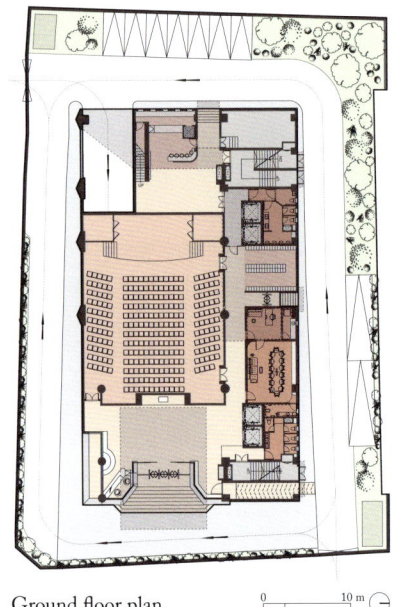
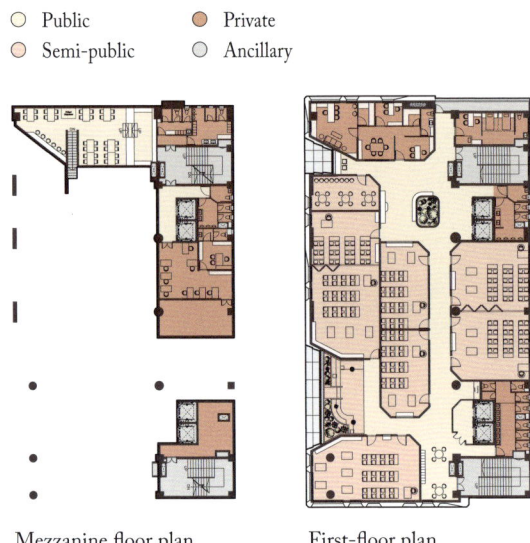

○ Public ● Private
● Semi-public ○ Ancillary

Mezzanine floor plan   First-floor plan

Ground floor plan   0 ▬ 10 m

Transverse section   0 ▬ 6 m

   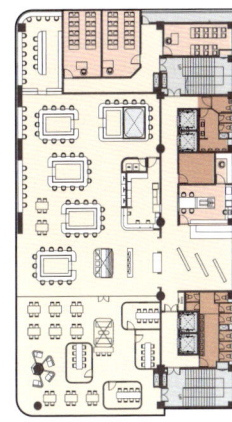

Second-floor plan   Third-floor plan   Fourth-floor plan   Fifth-floor plan

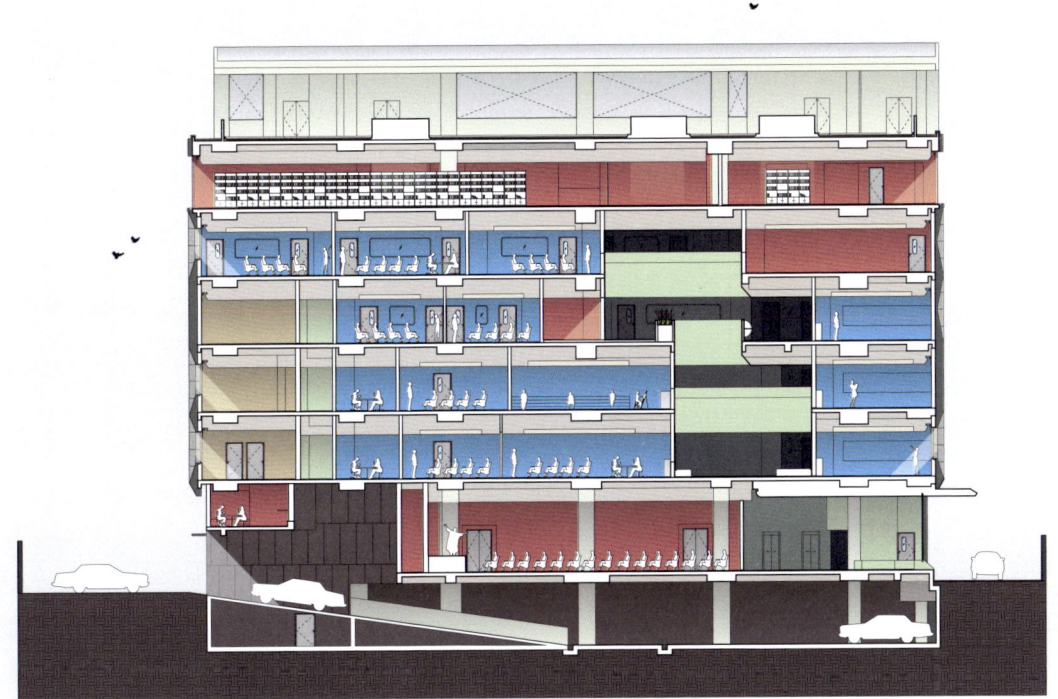

Longitudinal section

Modern High School International

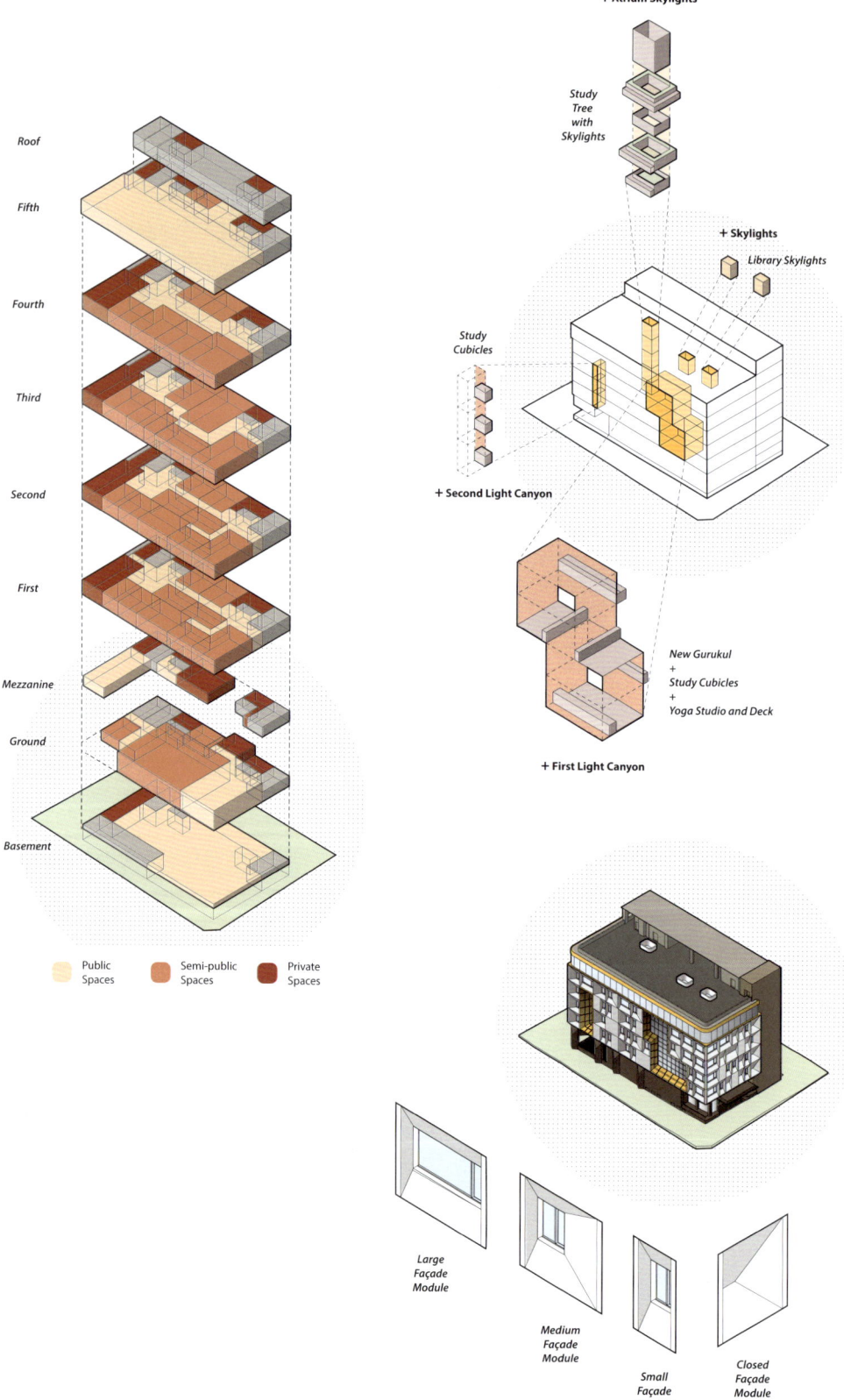

The new programmatic mix focuses on establishing dynamic relationships between student spaces and administration/teaching staff. For instance, the staff room is distributed across multiple levels to enhance student-teacher accessibility.

Each unique floor plate features a distinct programmatic distribution, encouraging student movement and creating a vibrant atmosphere throughout the building. Formal academic programs are seamlessly integrated with informal spaces such as a maker's workshop, exhibition space, yoga/exercise room, multipurpose studio, study nooks, and communal discussion areas to foster both conditioned and cognitive learning.

Moreover, the learning commons are strategically expanded to create intimate pockets of spaces by merging corridors and rearranging the placement of surrounding classrooms, resulting in winding circulation paths with various nooks. At the building's apex, an entire floor plate is dedicated to a state-of-the-art library with quiet and general discussion zones. The quiet zone includes discussion pods for individuals and groups, providing access to multimedia resources and facilitating meetings.

A continuous glazed ribbon of fenestration across three sides offers students a contextual view of the city while reading or studying in natural daylight. Adjacent to the library is an event space designated for functions like student exhibitions or workshops by esteemed guests and alumni. The library is envisioned as both an active facilitator and a receptacle for knowledge transfer, serving both students and the broader community.

Two "Light Canyons" are carved into the building mass, with an additional Light Canyon inserting itself down the middle, forming a naturally lit atrium. These canyons create staggered communal spaces and offer the public glimpses of the school's activities through these apertures.

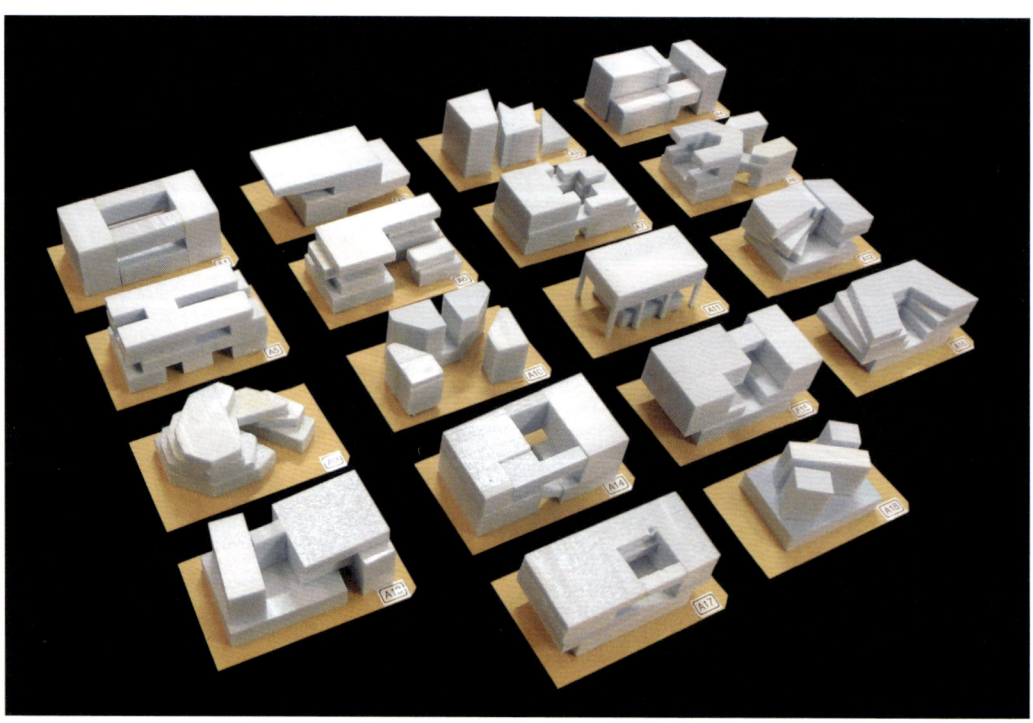

Cantilevered volumes articulate the main "Light Canyon" through cascading and staggered voids.

The primary Light Canyon features staggered discussion areas emerging from a biophilic classroom at the base level. This New Gurukul classroom was inspired by the rustic setting of traditional Indian Gurukul classes. Cantilevered platforms visually unite across different levels, while cascading voids take inspiration from natural canyon formations.

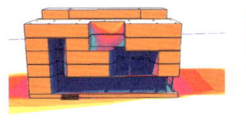
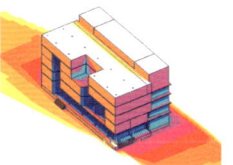
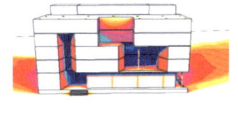
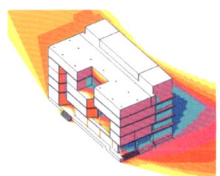

Summer Solar Simulation of selected massing models

Winter Solar Simulation of selected massing models

Modern High School International

The secondary Light Canyon introduces a tapered slot of light from the south, leading to the "Light Atrium." This bathes the atrium, fittingly named the Study Tree due to its patterned balustrades resembling branches, in natural light across five levels. The Study Tree area provides both communal discussion niches and individual study desks.

To achieve programmatic flexibility and introduce structural innovation on the south façade, the vertical services and circulation stacks were relocated to the north side. Additionally, structural engineering included the implementation of five post-tensioned beams capable of spanning up to 45 feet (14 meters) from the southern part of the building. This design choice resulted in a column-free environment for the multipurpose hall, a majority of classrooms, and the learning commons.

Creating a 45-foot (14-meter) column-free space on the north façade required post-tensioning of concrete beams. Stainless-steel tendons were placed within conduits and tensioned using hydraulic jacks and anchorage blocks before the concrete sets.

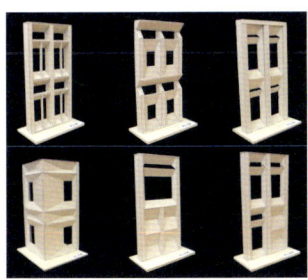

Exploring daylight openings and façade geometry through physical models.

The structural configuration not only allowed increased exposure to natural daylight from the south but also utilized cantilevered platforms to selectively filter direct sunlight into the common areas of the building. The strategically carved-out spaces, validated by solar radiance simulation studies, contribute to thermally comfortable enclosures, creating a conducive environment for students to gather throughout the day.

Given the persistent urban challenges of traffic noise and air pollution, the decision to glaze these Light Canyons was imperative. The primary goal was to establish an acoustically suitable environment with clean air, all while maintaining a visual connection to the city context through expansive fenestrations.

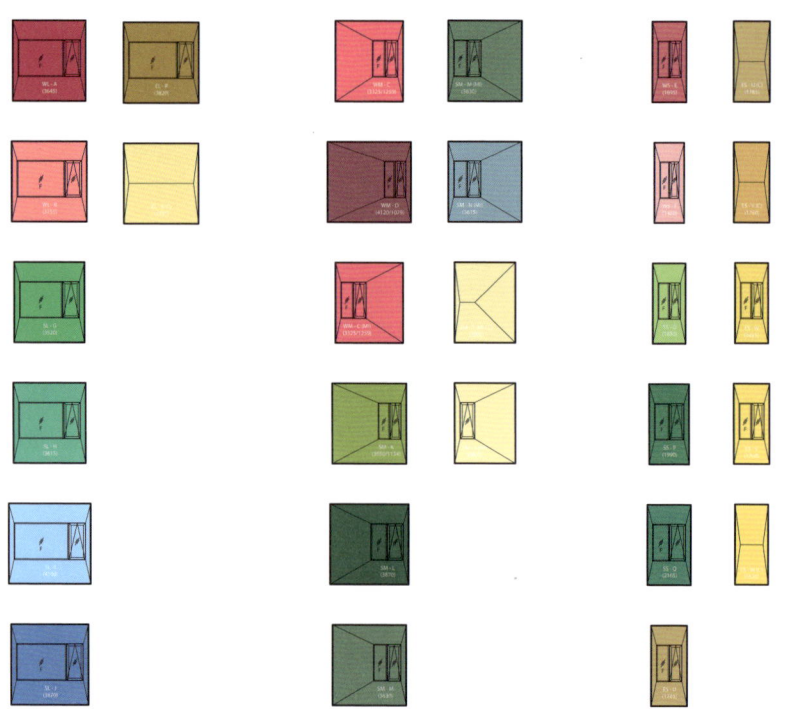

Large façade modules   Medium façade modules   Small façade modules

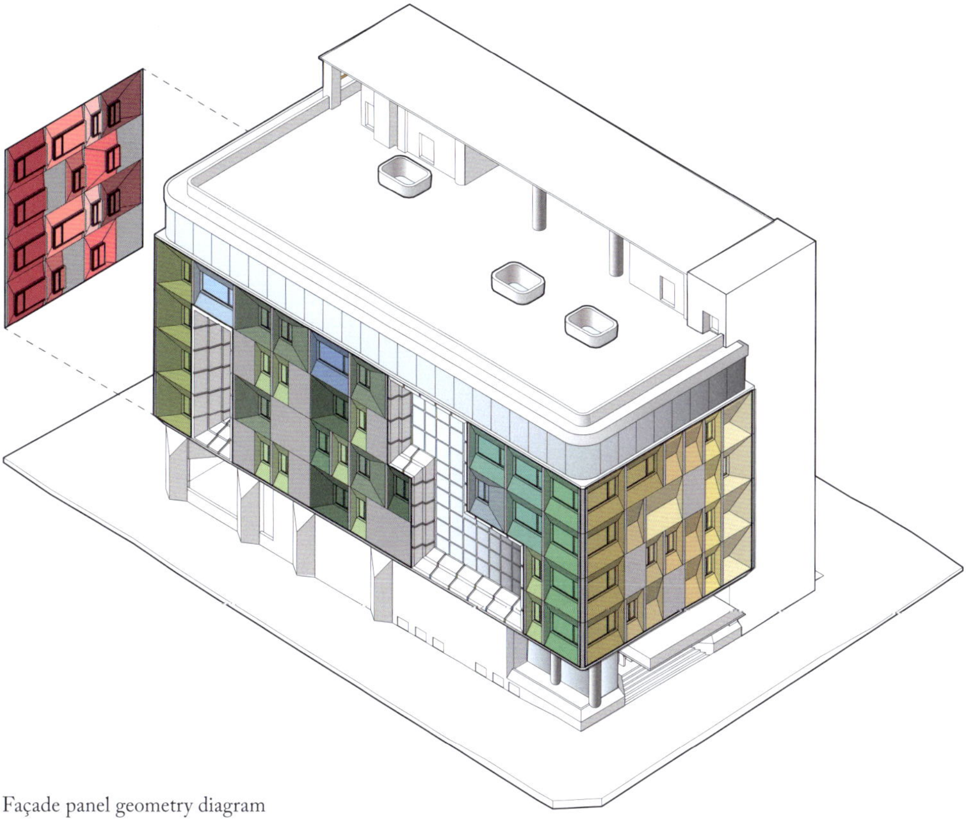

Façade panel geometry diagram

An aluminum framework was installed to support the ceramic paneled façade.

The primary façade envelops the building on three sides using inclined ceramic panels. The vertical air gap within the ventilated light-colored façade serves to insulate the building from direct solar radiation, prevent condensation build-up, and reflect the majority of the incoming sunlight. The façade, segmented into twenty-nine large modular types, is designed to optimize natural daylight penetration into the classrooms. Additionally, these inclined surfaces, coupled with recessed double-glazed windows, are strategically articulated to mitigate direct glare. The inclined form of these modules also addresses the client's practical request to minimize ledges for birds to perch, considered a nuisance in the city's context with their incessant droppings and chatter.

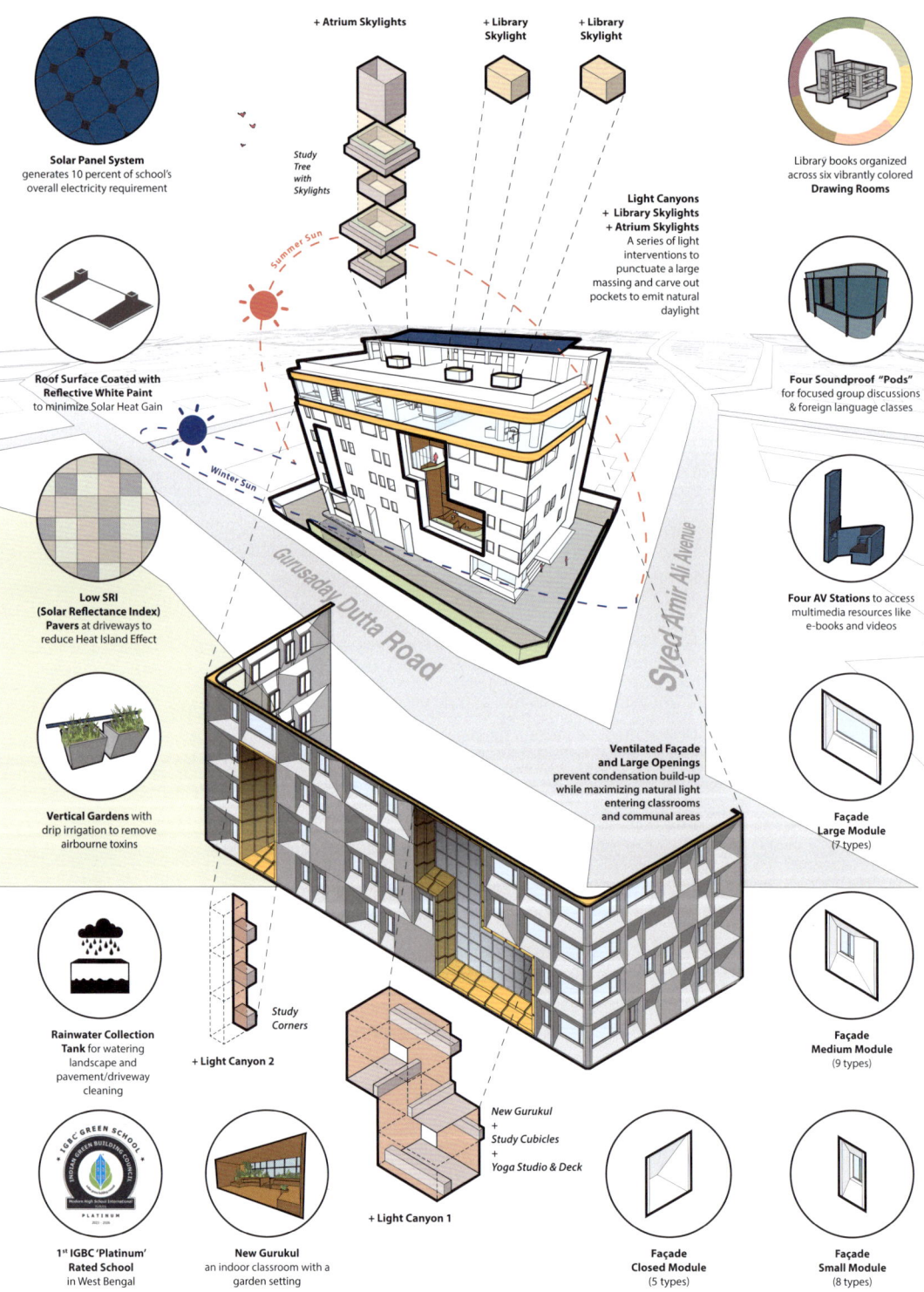

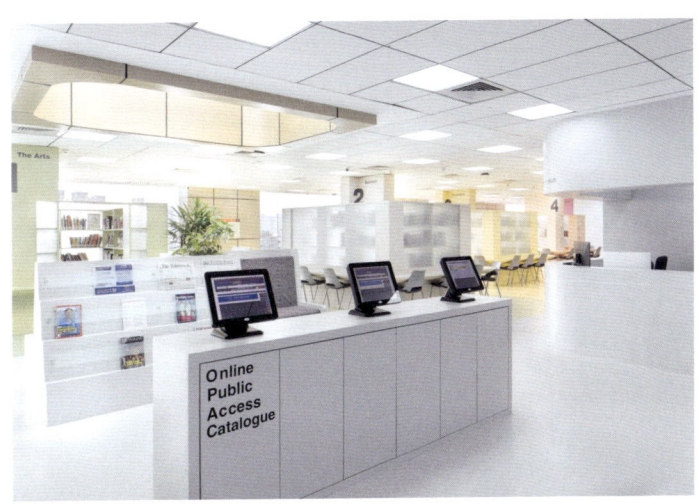

The school's commitment to sustainability and adherence to green building practices were integral from the initial design phase. The Indian Green Building Council's (IGBC) comprehensive sustainable strategies were diligently incorporated, leading the school to achieve the prestigious Platinum Mark (first in West Bengal state). Implemented strategies encompass sustainable water practices, promotion of healthy indoor air quality, utilization of eco-friendly school materials (pavers with low solar radiance index [SRI] to reduce heat island effect), installing clean energy equipment (solar panels), rainwater harvesting collection tanks, and integration of green education into the curriculum (hands-on workshops on sustainable innovations).

The entire building is envisioned as a showcase, allowing students to actively educate themselves in real time about green building strategies and practices.

The new Modern High School International aspires to be a "beacon of knowledge" by providing an environment shaped by both natural light and modern educational pedagogies.

"We are privileged to embark on design journeys with our clients and consultants, as a collective experience to explore market demands, environment sustainability, design technology, and socio-cultural landscapes with the hope of creating built environments that resonate with our design values."

Lo-Hi Tech Material Research
Primitive Materials: Future Frontiers

Lo-Hi Tech is all about leveraging the best of both worlds—embracing high and low technologies to craft innovative hybrid solutions that are not only efficient and sustainable but also address pressing environmental issues and improve human living conditions.

The research demonstrates the immense potential for sustainable solutions to contemporary challenges by combining Asian primitive materials with both modern and ancient technology. Additionally, it highlights the convergence of traditional craftsmanship with innovative techniques.

Our research focuses on two main building material systems:

Ke-Sol System (KSS)—Kenaf Fiber Biocomposites x Solar Panel System

The Ke-Sol System (KSS) seamlessly blends the strength of Kenaf fibers in lightweight biocomposite roof tiles with custom solar panels. Through a meticulous process involving high thermal pressure, Kenaf fiber mats are molded into robust yet lightweight roof panels. These panels are then integrated with monocrystalline solar panels, creating an innovative roof tile capable of generating clean energy through its modular and tiltable configurations. This integration showcases a harmonious fusion of nature and technology.

How does TCS work?

Sand particles gently release water into terra-cotta tiles, effectively cooling the surface and absorbing heat from the air. This process optimizes water usage and lowers the air temperature by 44°F (6.5°C), reducing the reliance on air conditioning.

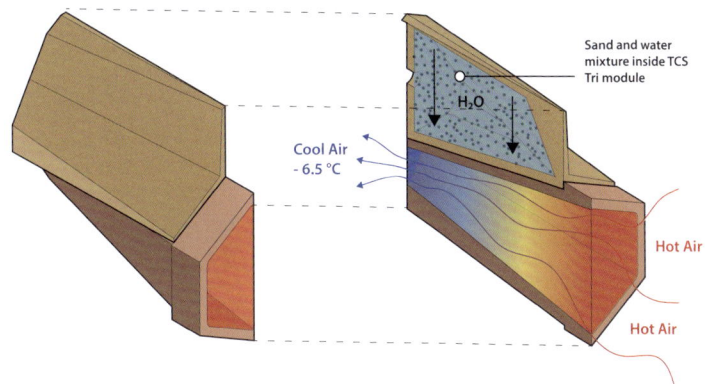

Terra-Cool System (TCS)—Terra-cotta x Evaporative Cooling Water + Sand Filter System

The Terra-Cool System (TCS) harnesses the natural properties of abundant terra-cotta, drawing inspiration from ancient refrigeration (Zeer pots) and irrigation (Olla Pots) techniques. Comprising two main structural modules—Hex and Tri components—the Hex converts hot air into cool air, while the Tri serves as a water tank, supplying water to the surrounding Hex.

By integrating terra-cotta with innovative technology, TCS forms a wall system capable of reducing air temperatures by an impressive 44 degrees Farenheit (6.5 degrees Celsius). This temperature drop is attributed to three key factors: the inherent cooling properties of terra-cotta, a meticulously designed form to maximize air and water flow, and the cooling effect driven by water evaporation. Furthermore, Computer Fluid Dynamics (CFD) simulations refine the design for optimal evaporative cooling performance.

Future Primitives-Use Case Scenario

We envision a future in which material systems effortlessly transition between shelter and vehicular infrastructure, transcending borders. The fundamental premise of our research is the seamless integration of the built environment with vehicles, including energy sources and sustainable materials. One relevant scenario involves creating sustainable shelter infrastructure for Electric Vehicle (EV) charging stations. These structures not only reduce ambient temperatures but also harness solar energy for localized lighting during the night.

Studio SKLIM
Transforming Design Boundaries, Creating Sustainable Futures

Studio SKLIM is an architectural design practice committed to pushing the boundaries of the built environment, design, and material exploration to craft transformative spaces. With a multidisciplinary approach, Studio SKLIM consistently challenges traditional norms, fostering innovation in its design concepts. Sustainability lies at the core of the practice, as it integrates sustainable strategies and future-proof primitive materials for contemporary applications. Based in Singapore, the studio also operates in India.

The firm's work has garnered extensive media coverage in international publications such as Thames & Hudson, Frame, Domus, Gestalten, Braun, Routledge, Images Publications, Links, Laurence King, and Phaidon. Particularly noteworthy is its residential project, Hansha Reflection House, which earned a place among Phaidon's distinguished "400 most influential, innovative, and awe-inspiring houses" in its renowned publication, *Houses*. The firm's projects have also graced the pages of leading online publications including *Designboom*, *Dezeen*, *ArchDaily*, *INDESIGN*, *Monocle*, and *Financial Times*.

Furthermore, Studio SKLIM's reach extends to prestigious exhibition venues worldwide, including Dongdaemun Design Plaza (Seoul's Design Museum), the Palazzo Morra (European Cultural Centre) in Venice, The Design Exchange (Canada's Design Museum) in Toronto, The Centre for Architecture (American Institute of Architects) in New York, and the Urban Redevelopment Authority (URA) Centre in Singapore. Additionally, their work has been featured on HGTV's architectural program *Extreme Homes*.

Currently, Studio SKLIM is actively engaged in architectural and design projects across the Asia Pacific region, with a track record of endeavors spanning Singapore, Japan, Thailand, South Korea, China, India, and Saudi Arabia.

Kevin Lim

The founding principal of Studio SKLIM, Kevin Lim, leads an award-winning interior and architectural design firm headquartered in Singapore, with notable projects spanning Singapore, Japan, China, and India. With the early influence of William Lim, one of Singapore's pioneering architects, Kevin's career trajectory has seen him gain experience across London, Singapore, and Beijing, collaborating with renowned international practices like the Office for Metropolitan Architecture (OMA) founded by Rem Koolhaas.

Kevin Lim frequently shares his insights at various events; from being a keynote speaker at Design Dialogues organized by the Indian Institute of Architects, Palakkad and Hyundai's ZER01NE Creators Talks in Seoul, to informal events like Pecha Kucha, Tokyo. Kevin's presence resonates across diverse platforms. Notably, he has contributed to creative initiatives like Heineken's Open Design Explorations for London Design Week and Hyundai's ZER01NE Creator program. He has served as a guest critic at local universities, and will run a design studio at the Department of Architecture, National University of Singapore from 2025.

Kevin Lim holds the AA Diploma from the Architectural Association in London and a Bachelor degree in Architecture from the National University of Singapore. Kevin is also an accredited professional of the India Green Building Council (IGBC).

Accolades

Awards

2024

Seoul Design Award 2024, Finalist: Lo-Hi Tech. Primitive Materials: Future Frontiers

Taipei Design Award 2024, Industrial Design, Finalist: Lo-Hi Tech. Primitive Materials: Future Frontiers

INDE Awards 2024, The Object, Honorable Mention: Lo-Hi Tech: Terra-Cool System

ZER01NE (Hyundai Motor Group) Creative Talent Platform 2024: Lo-Hi Tech. The New Primitive Hut

2023

ZER01NE (Hyundai Motor Group) Creative Talent Platform 2023: Lo-Hi Tech. Primitive Materials: Future Frontiers

Indian Green Building Council (IGBC) 2023 –Platinum Standard, Green Schools Rating System (New Schools): Modern High School International

INDE Awards 2023, The Learning Space, Shortlist: +Pavilion

2022

INDE Awards 2022, The Work Space, Shortlist: 9-15 Deloitte Center for the Edge

International Federation of Interior Architects/ Designers (IFI) Design Distinction Awards 2022, Play Category, Bronze: Voids Café

2021

Singapore Interior Design Awards (SIDA) 2021, Best in Workspace Design–Floor Area ≥ 500m², Gold (Completed & Luminary): 9-15 Deloitte Center for the Edge

Singapore Interior Design Awards (SIDA) 2021, Best in F&B Design–Cafe Spaces, Gold, (Completed & Luminary): Voids Café

Architecture MasterPrize 2021: Interior– Workplaces Category, Honorable Mention: 9-15 Deloitte Center for the Edge

Good Design Research Recipient 2021 – DesignSingapore Council: Kenopy (Kenaf Biocomposite Architectural Tiles) in collaboration with Affordable Pte Ltd

2020

Architecture MasterPrize 2020, Commercial Interior Category, Winner: Voids Café

INDE Awards 2020, The Social Space, Shortlist: Voids Café

2019

Architecture MasterPrize 2019, Interior– Workplaces Category, Honorable Mention: Verdant Spine Office

A' Design Award 2018–2019, Architecture, Building & Structure Design Category, Gold Award: Hansha Reflection House

A' Design Award 2018–2019, Interior Space and Exhibition Design Category, Silver Award: Verdant Spine Office

2018

Architecture MasterPrize 2018: Interior– Commercial Category, Honorable Mention: Brick Bakery

Architecture MasterPrize 2018: Interior–Retail Category, Honorable Mention: Rattan Clouds

Architecture MasterPrize 2018: Interior– Residential Category, Honorable Mention: Ombré Patchwork Apartment

2017
International Design Awards 2017: Interior–Conceptual Category, Honorable Mention: Rattan Clouds

Exhibitions

ZEROINE Day 2024
Lo-Hi Tech. The New Primitive Hut
Organised by ZERO1NE (Hyundai Motor Group), Peaches D8NE, Seoul, South Korea, 23rd–27th October 2024

Seoul Design 2023
Studio SKLIM: The Techne of Things
Organized and Supported by Seoul Design Foundation, Supported by DesignSingapore, Dongdaemun Design Plaza, Seoul, South Korea, 24th October–2nd November 2023

ZEROINE Day 2023
Lo-Hi Tech. Primitive Materials: Future Frontiers
Organized by ZERO1NE (Hyundai Motor Group), S Factory, Seoul, South Korea, 19th–22nd October 2023

Kenopy: Good Design Research Showcase
Organized by DesignSingapore, Pop-up Gallery, National Design Centre, Singapore, 15th July–10th August 2022

Venice Biennial Exhibition: Time Space Existence
Organized by European Cultural Centre (ECC), Palazzo Mora, Venice, Italy 22nd May–21st November 2021

A' Winners' Exhibition
Organized by A' Design Awards, "MOOD" Ex Chiesa di San Francesco, Como, Italy, 10th June–31st July 2019

Homegrown: A Singapore Design Consciousness
Organized by MKPL Architects, Urban Redevelopment Authority (URA) Atrium, Singapore, 29th March–15th April 2016

Considering the Quake: Seismic Design on the Edge
Organized by Centre for Architecture–American Institute of Architects (New York Chapter), Curated by Dr Effie Bouras and Professor Ghyslaine McClure, New York, USA, 13th February–26th May 2014

Considering the Quake: Seismic Design on the Edge
Organized by Design Exchange–Canada's Design Museum, Curated by Dr Effie Bouras and Professor Ghyslaine McClure, Toronto, Canada, 13th September–13th November 2012

Broadcast Media

Extreme Homes: Bubbles, Bottles & Bookcases
Commissioned by Home & Gardens TV (HGTV), USA, Produced by Pioneer Productions, UK, First telecast on 8th November 2012

Acknowledgments

We extend our deepest appreciation and profound gratitude to Smt. Nirmala Birla, Professor Ciro Najle, Mr Duleesha Kulasooriya, Mr Scott Taylor, and Dr Woon Tien Wei for generously dedicating their time to penning testimonials and sharing invaluable insights about our work. Their contributions have added immeasurable value to this book.

We wish to extend our utmost gratitude to Orient Electric and Greenlam Industries for their invaluable sponsorship and unwavering support, without which the production of this monograph would not have been possible. Thank you also to 42 Degrees Asia for your support.

I am eternally grateful to the late Professor William Lim Siew Wai for his early mentorship and for instilling in me the spirit of creative collaboration. Special thanks to Mr Kong Shee Chong for laying the unconventional foundations of my early architectural education. I extend my sincere gratitude to Professor Ciro Najle for introducing me to the principles of consistency, obsession, and discipline in diagramming, and for challenging and reshaping my architectural perspective. My heartfelt appreciation goes to Professor Hanif Kara for being an inspiration in the exploration of structural forms and performance-based solutions.

Special thanks to Ashwin Bafna for his dedicated involvement in our projects and his ability to offer unique perspectives. We would also like to express gratitude to the many other collaborators who have contributed to our projects.

Our sincere gratitude to the following entities for engaging with us and providing the platform to express our strengths: Cairnhill Law, Deloitte Center for the Edge, DesignSingapore, Emporium of Modern Man, Grace Espresso, Kang family, Matsumoto family, Modern High School International, the Swiss Embassy Singapore, and ZER01NE (Hyundai Motor Group).

We are fortunate to have collaborated with the following individuals, who generously lent their talent, expertise, and unwavering commitment to our projects: Bimal Mistry, Chetan Agarwal, Devanshu Daga, Duleesha Kulasooriya, Indra Bansal, Francis Cheng, GS Agarwal, K C Tan, Laurent Corpataux, Machiko Nakamura, Manish Kakkar, Rajesh Selvaganapathy, Sanjay Nandi, Suresh Sinha, Tim Tan, Tommy Kang, Wong Siew Huey, Yuri Tan, and Yvonne Zhang.

For seeing our projects through a different lens and expressing them with their own unique perspectives, we extend our appreciation to: Hitesh Toolsidass, Jaume Albert Martí, Khoo Guo Jie, Ong Chan Hao, and the late Jeremy San Tzer Ning.

For being extremely supportive and understanding in this publication journey and for the prestigious selection of our work: Honorine Le Fleur, Ryan Marshall, Jeanette Wall, Nicole Boehringer, Gina Tsarouhas, and the team at Images Publishing.

Special thanks to my parents for their unconditional support in nurturing my passion for architecture and design from its inception. To the Nakamura family, your unwavering encouragement has been invaluable. ありがとう、お父さん。I am grateful to Machiko for her patience and compassion throughout this journey. Lastly, heartfelt appreciation to my two children, Soui and Horii, for their assistance with the abstract patterns of the book and for being enduring wellsprings of inspiration.

Without the kind support of these individuals and projects, this book would not have been possible. We extend our sincere gratitude to everyone we reached out to for comments on various aspects of the book. Our heartfelt appreciation goes to those who have been with us on this journey, including those whose names we might have inadvertently omitted.

Project Credits

Voids Café (pp26–39)
Location: Singapore
Completion: 2019
Area: 28m²
Team: Kevin Lim, Ashwin Bafna, Svasti Agrawal
Client: Grace Espresso
Photography: Khoo Guo Jie / Studio SKLIM

Deloitte Center for the Edge (pp40–57)
Location: Singapore
Completion: 2020
Area: 32m²
Team: Kevin Lim, Ashwin Bafna
Consultants: Vitra (Furniture); Affordable Abodes (Kenafcrete lamp); Lighting (42 Degrees Asia)
Client: Deloitte Center for the Edge (Asia-Pacific)
Photography: Khoo Guo Jie / Studio SKLIM

Hansha Reflection House (pp58–81)
Location: Nagoya, Japan
Completion: 2011
Area: 124m²
Team: Kevin Lim, Machiko Nakamura
Collaborators: Federico Mira (3D)
Client: Matsumoto Family
Builder: Sakae Advanced Housing Technology
Structure: Shelter inc. KES System
Photography: Jeremy San / Studio SKLIM

Rattan Clouds (pp82–91)
Location: Singapore
Completion: 2015
Area: 68m²
Team: Kevin Lim, Beatrice Ong
Client: Emporium of Modern Man
Photography: Khoo Guo Jie

Verdant Spine Office (pp92–105)
Location: Singapore
Completion: 2019
Area: 135m²
Team: Kevin Lim, Ashwin Bafna
Client: Cairnhill Law
Photography: Khoo Guo Jie

+ Pavilion (pp106–19)
Location: Singapore
Completion: 2022
Area: 85m²
Team: Kevin Lim, Ashwin Bafna
Partners/Collaborators: Affordable Abodes; Deloitte (Singapore); EHL Campus (Singapore); Haring Timber Technology; Hilti; Marina Barrage; Nespresso; UBS; Vitra
Consultants/Construction: Keon Consult; TopZone E&C; Pleo Cre8tions; HAM Creation
Client: Embassy of Switzerland in Singapore
Photography: Ong Chan Hao / Haring Timber Technology / Studio SKLIM

Brick Bakery (pp 120–33)
Location: Singapore
Completion: 2014
Area: 100m²
Team: Kevin Lim, Irwin Ho
Client: Bread and Hearth
Photography: Khoo Guo Jie

Ombré Patchwork Apartment (pp 134–49)
Location: Singapore
Completion: 2017
Area: 184m²
Team: Kevin Lim, Josh Punpeng Pattarapol
Client: Kang Family
Photography: Jaume Albert Martí

Bamboo Umbrella Pavilions (pp 150–57)
Location: Bangkok, Thailand
Design: 2018
Area: 972m²
Team: Kevin Lim, Josh Punpeng Pattarapol
Client: Confidential
Photography: Studio SKLIM

Modern High School International (pp 158–81)
Location: Kolkata, India
Completion: 2023
Area: 8,000m²
Team: Kevin Lim, Ashwin Bafna, Josh Punpeng Pattarapol, Svasti Agrawal, Suruchi Agrawal, Aaron Lee, Zakhran Khan, Desmond Lee
Collaborators: Kothari & Associates (Kolkata) and Bimal Mistry (Partner in Charge), Chetan Agarwal, G.S Agarwal, Suraj Sinha, Indra Bansal, Sanjay Nandi, S.P.A. Consultants, Balaji Electrical, Rajesh Selvaganapathy, Aqua Utility Designs Management, Geotests Engineers, Godrej & Boyce, MFAR Constructions, AS Group
Client: Modern High School International (CK Birla Group)
Photography: Hitesh Toolsidass / Studio SKLIM

Lo-Hi Tech Materials Research (pp 184–89)
Location: Seoul, South Korea
Completion: 2023
Area: 57m²
Team: Kevin Lim, Ashwin Bafna
Collaborators: Ong Chan Hao, Yvonne Zhang, Athun K R, Livingstan S, Manoj S, Sivagnanam V, Prabhu A, Sanmugam S, Sakthivel S, Ganesha Moorthi C, Nikhin K, Arun S, Devanshu D, Gurav J
Client: ZER01NE (Hyundai Motor Group)
Photography: Ong Chan Hao / ZER01NE / Athun K R / Studio SKLIM

Published in Australia in 2025 by
The Images Publishing Group Pty Ltd
ABN 89 059 734 431

Offices

Melbourne
Waterman Business Centre
Suite 64, Level 2 UL40
1341 Dandenong Road
Chadstone, VIC 3148
Australia
Tel: +61 3 8564 8122

New York
6 West 18th Street 4B
New York City, NY 10011
United States
Tel: +1 212 645 1111

Shanghai
6F, Building C, 838 Guangji Road
Hongkou District, Shanghai 200434
China
Tel: +86 021 31260822

books@imagespublishing.com
www.imagespublishing.com

Copyright © The Images Publishing Group Pty Ltd 2025
The Images Publishing Group Reference Number: 1678

All rights reserved. Apart from any fair dealing for the purposes of private study, research, criticism or review as permitted under the Copyright Act, no part of this publication may be reproduced, stored in a retrieval system or transmitted in any form by any means, electronic, mechanical, photocopying, recording or otherwise, without the written permission of the publisher.

All photography is attributed in the Project Credits on pages 194–95 with the following exceptions. Cover: Hitesh Toolsidass (Modern High School International); Back cover (clockwise from top left): Hitesh Toolsidass (Modern High School International); Jeremy San (Hansha Reflection House); Khoo Guo Jie (Voids Café); Ong Chan Hao (Lo-Hi Tech Material Research); Back flap portrait: Hitesh Toolsidass (Kevin Lim); Pages 20–1: Studio SKLIM; Page 193: Hitesh Toolsidass (Kevin Lim)

 A catalogue record for this book is available from the National Library of Australia

Title: Studio SKLIM: Evolving Techne
Author: Kevin Lim, Studio SKLIM
ISBN: 9781864709551

This title was commissioned in IMAGES' Melbourne office and produced as follows:
Editorial Danielle Hampshire, Jeanette Wall, *Graphic design/Project management* Ryan Marshall, *Art direction/production* Nicole Boehringer, *Senior editorial* Georgia (Gina) Tsarouhas

Printed on 140gsm Da Dong Woodfree paper (FSC®) in China by Artron Art Group

IMAGES has included on its website a page for special notices in relation to this and its other publications. Please visit www.imagespublishing.com

Every effort has been made to trace the original source of copyright material contained in this book. The publishers would be pleased to hear from copyright holders to rectify any errors or omissions.

The information and illustrations in this publication have been prepared and supplied by Studio SKLIM. While all reasonable efforts have been made to ensure accuracy, the publishers do not, under any circumstances, accept responsibility for errors, omissions and representations, express or implied.